SPOTLIGHT

D1553150

GEORGIAN BAY & COTTAGE COUNTRY

CAROLYN B. HELLER

Contents

GEORGIAN BAY & COTTAGE COUNTRY

GEORGIAN BAY AND COTTAGE COUNTRY

If you're looking for a getaway to the outdoors, whether to be soothed and healed or exhilarated by the adventure, head to Georgian Bay and Ontario's "Cottage Country."

The eastern finger of Lake Huron, Georgian Bay is 320 kilometers (200 miles) long and 80 kilometers (50 miles) wide, and it's surrounded by some of Ontario's most spectacular scenery. The Georgian Bay region has three national parks, several large provincial parks, dramatic rock formations, Caribbean-blue water, and a network of red-and-white lighthouses standing guard along the shore. There are ski slopes and canoe routes, as well as the world's longest freshwater beach, and offshore, the bay waters are dotted with more than 30,000 islands and some of the finest scuba diving in the north. The region is a hugely popular destination for hikers, too, since it contains the northern portions of the Bruce Trail, Canada's longest hiking route.

You won't want to miss the stunning Bruce Peninsula, with its unusual rock formations, offshore islands, and network of hiking trails. The Georgian Bay Islands National Park is the gateway to the 30,000 islands region, and splurging on a floatplane tour is a new level of thrill. Winter sports enthusiasts should head to the Blue Mountains, Ontario's top ski and snowboarding region. If you prefer history and culture with your outdoor adventures, the towns of Midland, Penetanguishene, and Parry Sound will oblige.

To escape the city's frenzy, many Torontonians head north to Cottage Country. Cottage Country begins just 100 kilometers (60 miles)

© CAROLYN B. HELLER

HIGHLIGHTS

LOOK FOR ◖ TO FIND RECOMMENDED SIGHTS, ACTIVITIES, DINING, AND LODGING.

◖ **Bruce Peninsula National Park:** This national park is among Ontario's most beautiful settings. Its intricate rock formations, turquoise waters, and more than 40 species of orchids draw hikers, kayakers, and other nature lovers (page 13).

◖ **The Bruce Trail:** This iconic Canadian hiking route stretches 845 kilometers (525 miles) from the Niagara region to the end of the Bruce Peninsula (page 14).

◖ **Fathom Five National Marine Park:** One of only three national marine conservation areas in Canada, this marine park is best known for its distinctive "flowerpot" rock formations. It also has some of the finest scuba diving in North America (page 17).

◖ **Sainte-Marie Among the Hurons:** This historic village "reimagines" the first European settlement in Ontario, where French Jesuits lived and worked with the native Wendat (Huron) people in the 1600s (page 36).

◖ **The Georgian Bay Islands National Park:** Of the thousands of islands that dot Georgian Bay, 63 are protected in this island national park. Visit for a day of hiking and swimming, or try an "all-inclusive" camping experience (page 41).

◖ **Flight-Seeing:** The most thrilling way to take in Georgian Bay's 30,000 Islands is on a floatplane tour. Soar above the bay by day or take a romantic sunset flight – complete with champagne (page 45).

◖ **Killbear Provincial Park:** This waterfront area near Parry Sound offers granite cliffs, sandy beaches, and a lovely destination for hiking, canoeing, swimming, and camping (page 47).

◖ **Canoeing in Algonquin Provincial Park:** Ontario's largest provincial park is one of the province's best destinations for canoeing, whether you're paddling on the numerous lakes and rivers or taking a multiday trip across the backcountry (page 67).

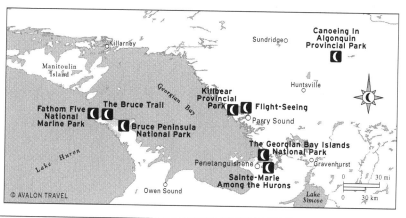

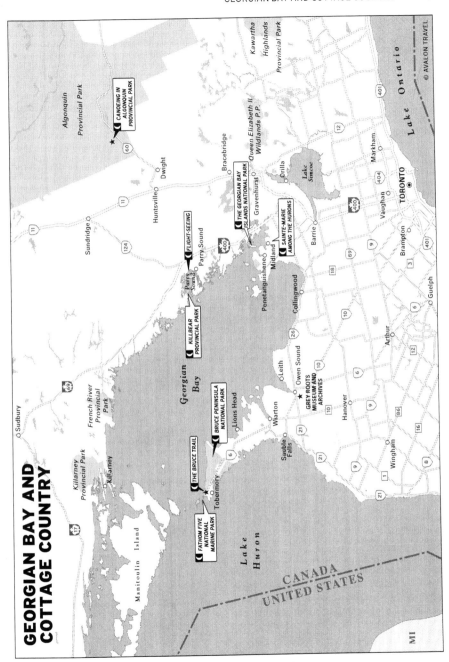

north of Toronto and includes Gravenhurst, Bracebridge, and Huntsville. Dotted with inland lakes, ski hills, and waterfront towns along Lake Muskoka and numerous smaller lakes, this region offers numerous opportunities for outdoor adventure and relaxation. Don't-miss attractions include Algonquin Provincial Park, one of Ontario's largest protected green spaces. Algonquin is one of the province's highlights; visit for a day or a week and take a short hike, paddle across an inland lake, or set out on a multiday wilderness adventure.

PLANNING YOUR TIME

This region is packed with outdoors highlights, but many attractions and services around Georgian Bay and Cottage Country don't begin operation till mid- or late May and close in mid-October after the Canadian

Thanksgiving weekend. One exception is the Blue Mountains, which draws winter visitors for skiing and snowboarding.

For a long weekend, do a quick tour of the **Bruce Peninsula,** ski or snowboard at **Blue Mountain,** pair a visit to **Midland**'s historic sights with a day trip to the **Georgian Bay Islands National Park,** or base yourself in **Parry Sound** and explore the nearby provincial parks. A weekend trip could also take you to **Algonquin** for a relaxing getaway to the Muskokas.

You can easily spend a week exploring the Bruce Peninsula, particularly if you want to hike sections of the Bruce Trail or scuba-dive in the **Fathom Five National Marine Park.** Between May and October, a ferry runs between the Bruce Peninsula and **Manitoulin Island,** for further exploration.

The Bruce Peninsula

From limestone cliffs to crystal blue waters to forested hiking trails and even a wide variety of orchids, the Bruce Peninsula's striking natural scenery is the main reason to visit this finger of land that juts out between Lake Huron and Georgian Bay. The must-see attractions are its two national parks—The Bruce Peninsula National Park and Fathom Five National Marine Park—located at the peninsula's north end, around the town of Tobermory. Yet beyond these natural attractions, it's the friendly, low-key atmosphere that draws vacationers. Though the region attracts plenty of visitors, it hasn't lost its small-town warmth, with people greeting each other on the street and on the trail.

For pre-trip research, check out the detailed **County of Bruce Tourism website** (www.explorethebruce.com), which lists vast amounts of information about the Bruce Peninsula and surrounding communities. Also pick up the extremely useful **Grey-Bruce Official Visitor Map** (www.explorethebruce.com) at information centers around

the region; it shows both major and minor roads across the peninsula.

TOBERMORY

To explore the Bruce Peninsula National Park and the Fathom Five National Marine Park, it's most convenient to base yourself in Tobermory, a pretty waterfront town at the northern tip of the Bruce Peninsula. Highway 6, the peninsula's main north–south road, ends in Tobermory.

National Park Visitor Centre

Start your visit at the National Park Visitor Centre (120 Chi Sin Tib Dek Rd., 519/596-2233, www.pc.gc.ca, adults $5.80, seniors $4.90, children $2.90), which has information about both Bruce Peninsula National Park and Fathom Five National Marine Park. You can watch a short film about the area's highlights and explore exhibits about the local ecology. In summer, a variety of interpretive programs, including guided hikes and children's activities, are offered; schedules are posted online at the

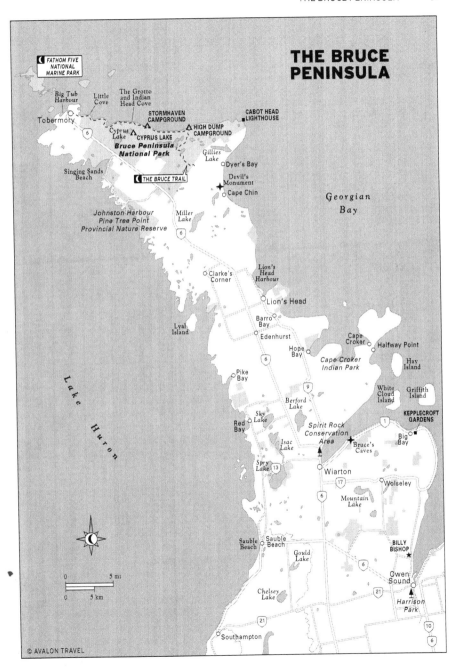

THE BRUCE PENINSULA

FATHOM FIVE
NATIONAL
MARINE PARK

Big Tub
Harbour
Little
Cove
The Grotto
and Indian
Head Cove

Tobermory

STORMHAVEN
CAMPGROUND

CABOT HEAD
LIGHTHOUSE

Cyprus
Lake
CYPRUS LAKE

HIGH DUMP
CAMPGROUND

**Bruce Peninsula
National Park**

Gillies
Lake

Dyer's Bay

Singing Sands
Beach

THE BRUCE TRAIL

Devil's
Monument
Cape Chin

*Georgian
Bay*

Johnston Harbour
Pine Tree Point
Provincial Nature Reserve

Miller
Lake

L a k e

Clarke's
Corner

Lion's
Head
Harbour

Lion's Head

Barro
Bay

H u r o n

Lyal
Island

Edenhurst

Hope
Bay

Cape
Croker
Halfway Point

*Cape Croker
Indian Park*

Hay
Island

Pike
Bay

White
Cloud
Island
Griffith
Island

Berford
Lake

KEPPLECROFT
GARDENS

Red
Bay
Ska
Lake

Spirit Rock
Conservation
Area

Big
Bay

Isac
Lake

Bruce's
Caves

Spry
Lake

Wiarton

Wolseley

Mountain
Lake

Sauble
Beach
Sauble
Beach

Gould
Lake

BILLY
BISHOP

Owen
Sound

Chelsey
Lake

Harrison
Park

Southampton

0   5 mi

0   5 km

© AVALON TRAVEL

ON THE LOOKOUT FOR LIGHTHOUSES

What is it about lighthouses that draw people like a beacon? If you're a lighthouse lover, the Lake Huron and Georgian Bay coasts are prime territory for lighthouse touring. Many of the region's lighthouses were built in the mid- to late 1800s or early 1900s during the heyday of Great Lakes shipping.

On Lake Huron, visit the **Chantry Island Light** (www.chantryisland.com) near Southampton and the **Kincardine Lighthouse** (www.sunsets.com), a lighthouse-turned-museum just a short walk from Kincardine's downtown. The Bruce Peninsula has several lighthouses, including the **Big Tub Lighthouse** in Tobermory, the **Cabot Head Lighthouse and Museum** (www.cabothead.ca), the **Lion's Head Lighthouse** on Lion's Head Beach, and the **Cape Croker Lighthouse** at the tip of Cape Crocker, a First Nations reserve. On Flowerpot Island in the Fathom Five National Marine Park, you can visit the **Flow-**erpot **Island Lightstation.** One of the most picturesque light stations is the **Killarney East Lighthouse,** on the bay near Killarney Provincial Park.

Today the lonely job of lighthouse keeper has generally gone the way of the dodo bird, as most lighthouse operations are now computerized. For a glimpse of old-fashioned lighthouse-keeping life, book a stay at **Cabot Head Lighthouse** (www.cabothead.ca), where you can spend a week as part of the assistant lightkeeper's program (late May-mid-Oct.). It's a working holiday where you help greet visitors to the lighthouse, assist in the gift shop, and pitch in with some housekeeping duties. For reservations, contact the **Friends of Cabot Head** (mailing address: P.O. Box 233, Lion's Head, ON, N0H 1W0; email cabothead@hotmail.com). The lighthouse stays are quite popular, so make your plans well in advance.

---

center and on the Friends of the Bruce District Parks Association (www.castlebluff.com). If you plan to camp on Flowerpot Island in the Fathom Five Marine Park, or to scuba-dive in any of the park territory, you must register at the Visitor Centre before heading out.

The Visitor Centre is the northernmost point on the Bruce Trail. Check out the "sculpture" made from hikers' worn boots in the lobby and the **Bruce Trail Cairn** out front marking the end of the Bruce Trail. If you've hiked the entire trail, this is the spot to take your photo. Two hiking trails start at the center. It's an easy 800-meter (half-mile) walk to the **Little Dunks Bay Lookout.** The 3.5-kilometer (two-mile) **Burnt Point Loop Trail** meanders through the forest to Georgian Bay, where you can look out over the Fathom Five islands. Near the Visitor Centre is a 20-meter (65-foot) **Lookout Tower.** Climb the 112 steps for views out across the peninsula and the nearby islands.

Visitor Centre hours vary seasonally. From mid-July through early September, the center is open daily 8 A.M.–8 P.M. (and until 9 P.M. on Fri.). From early September through mid-October, hours are 10 A.M.–6 P.M. Sunday through Friday and 8 A.M.–6 P.M. Saturday. For the rest of the year, the center is open 10 A.M.–4 P.M. Tuesday through Saturday. The Visitor Centre is located about a 10-minute walk from Tobermory's Little Tub Harbour along a flat, partly paved section of the Bruce Trail. By car, look for the park sign on Highway 6, just south of town.

Little Tub Harbour

Most of Tobermory's shops and services are clustered around Little Tub Harbour. Boats to the Fathom Five islands leave from Little Tub, as do a variety of sightseeing cruises (mid-May–mid-Oct.) around Tobermory and the Fathom Five islands.

The two-hour Great Blue Heron glass-bottom boat tour, run by **Blue Heron Tours** (Little Tub Harbour, 519/596-2999, www.blueheronco.com, adults $35.31, seniors $33.37, children 4–12 $25.76), sails around Russel Island, Cove Island, the Otter Islands, and Flowerpot Island. You can do this two-hour tour as a sunset cruise for the same price.

G+S Watersports (8 Bay St. South, 519/596-2200, www.gswatersports.net) also offers sightseeing cruises. They run a two-hour Flowerpot Island Cruise ($25), a two-hour Cove Island Lighthouse Tour (also $25), and a 45-minute Sweepstakes Tour($15) to see the shipwrecks in Big Tub Harbour.

Big Tub Harbour
Tobermory has a second port area, known as Big Tub Harbour. The first lighthouse at Big Tub was constructed in 1885 to guide ships safely into port. The present-day **Big Tub Lighthouse,** a hexagonal tower that was automated in 1952, still performs that role at the harbor's mouth. The lighthouse isn't open to the public, but you can walk around the exterior and along the rocky shore. You can also swim or snorkel here.

The remains of two 19th-century ships lie in the shallow water of Big Tub Harbour. The **Sweepstakes,** a two-masted schooner, ran aground near Cove Island Lighthouse in 1885; the boat was towed to Big Tub Harbour, where it sank. The steamer **City of Grand Rapids** caught fire in 1907 while docked in Little Tub Harbour. The boat was towed out of the harbor to prevent the fire from spreading to other nearby ships; the burning ship then drifted into Big Tub Harbour and sank there.

You can see the shipwrecks on one of the boat tours out of Tobermory or on several of the Flowerpot Island boats. Scuba diving is allowed around the wrecks, but only at designated times, since boat traffic in the area can be heavy. Check with the National Park Visitor Centre (519/596-2233, www.pc.gc.ca) for details.

Entertainment and Shopping
Looking for a unique way to spend an evening? Storytellers Leslie Robbins-Conway and Paul Conway open their home to visitors as hosts of **Voyageur Storytelling: Country Supper**

Storytelling Concerts (56 Brinkman's Rd., Miller Lake, 519/795-7477, www.voyageurstorytelling.ca, Tues.–Sat., mid-June–early Sept., adults $46, seniors and students $42, children $36), pairing a multicourse home-cooked meal with a storytelling performance.

At the annual **Orchid Festival** (www.orchidfest.ca, late May), you can join guided orchid-viewing walks, take flower drawing or photography workshops, or learn more about the peninsula's orchid population. Check the website for a schedule, or stop into festival headquarters at the Bruce Peninsula National Park Visitor Centre (120 Chi Sin Tib Dek Rd., Tobermory, 519/596-2233).

Most of the shops around Little Tub Harbour sell T-shirts and other ordinary souvenirs. One exception is **Circle Arts** (14 Bay St., 519/596-2541, www.circlearts.com) and its sister location, **Circle Arts Too** (10 Bay St., 519/596-2543). These fine-art galleries showcase prints, paintings, sculpture, photographs, jewelry, textiles, one-of-a-kind furniture, and other works crafted by Canadian artists, many of whom have ties to the Bruce Peninsula. You might find everything from a $15 ceramic candleholder to a $20,000 painting. Both galleries are open mid-May to mid-October.

Accommodations
A number of motels and B&Bs are clustered around, or within walking distance of, Little Tub Harbour. Other accommodations dot Highway 6 south of town; if you don't want to take your car everywhere, try to stay near the harbor. In July and August, and on holiday weekends, even basic motel rooms go for over $100 per night; it's a good idea to book in advance, or at least arrive early in the day. The **Tobermory Chamber of Commerce** (www.tobermory.org) has a list of local accommodations on its website.

Inside this nondescript vinyl-sided house about a 15-minute walk from Little Tub Harbour is the surprisingly stylish **Molinari's B&B** (68 Water Dr., 877/596-1228, www.themolinaris.com, $115–125 d). The three contemporary guest rooms are done in richly hued textiles and outfitted with microwaves, fridges, coffeemakers, and small flat-screen TVs. Guests take their breakfast in the sleek industrial kitchen; there's no other common space, though, so it's not a sit-around-and-chat kind of lodging. Owners Maria and Bob, who relocated from Montreal after falling in love with the Bruce Peninsula during scuba-diving visits here, also run **Molinari's Espresso Bar and Italian Restaurant** (53 Bay St., 519/596-1228) in town. The B&B is open year-round; the restaurant is open May through October.

The friendly **Blue Bay Motel** (32 Bay St., 519/596-2392, www.bluebay-motel.com, May–mid-Oct., $130–160 d), right above Little Tub Harbour, has 16 basic but comfortable rooms with fridges and coffeemakers; the best are the renovated ones with more modern linens and wood floors, or the second-floor units with water views (the first-floor rooms face the parking lot). There's also a large three-bedroom suite with a full kitchen.

The **Maple Golf Inn** (22 Maple Golf Crescent, 519/596-8166, www.maplegolfinn.ca, $100–125 d, $145–175 suite), in a suburban home about a 10-minute drive south of Tobermory, is popular with hikers, since there's an access point to the Bruce Trail nearby. On the main floor are two comfortable rooms decorated in a modern country style, with quilts, wood floors, and private baths. Hosts Jill and Lawrence Stewart serve a full English breakfast, and guests can lounge in the living room, which looks onto the Cornerstone Golf Club. Downstairs, with a private entrance, is a family-friendly basement suite, which includes a living room with a sofa bed, a separate bedroom with king bed, and a kitchenette. The B&B is open year-round, but the downstairs suite, which has no central heating, is available only in milder weather.

Looking for a true get-away-from-it-all place? At **(E'Terra** (www.eterra.ca, $395–560 d), a sumptuous wood and stone manor house hidden in the woods, the phone number is unlisted, the property has no sign, and the owners won't divulge the address until

you make a reservation. The inn's philosophy is "eco-epicurean," pairing over-the-top luxury with environmental sensitivity. Four of the six guest rooms are two-story suites, and all have French linens, silk duvets, and heated flagstone floors. Guests can unwind in the spacious living room or in the cozy third-floor library and take a sauna or a dip in the saltwater pool. As you climb higher in the house, the vistas of Georgian Bay become more expansive, although the most striking views may be from the multilevel Douglas fir deck behind the building, tiered into the rocks above the water. You could drive to Tobermory in just a few minutes, but why would you want to leave?

Food

Most of Tobermory's dining options are in or near Little Tub Harbour, with a few other eateries along Highway 6.

Just south of town, in a little house off Highway 6, the **Little Tub Bakery** (4 Warner Bay Rd., 519/596-8399, www.littletubbakery.org, 9 A.M.–6 P.M. Mon.–Fri. in summer; call for off-season hours) is justifiably famous for their gooey butter tarts. The cinnamon rolls and freshly baked pies are also popular, or you can pick up a sandwich or homemade pizza for a picnic.

A Mermaid's Secret Café (7433 Hwy. 6, 519/596-8455, www.amermaidssecret.com, seasonal hours vary, $6–10), an eclectic eatery decorated in a cheerful chaos of Caribbean colors, serves some of the most interesting food in town. Besides organic fair-trade coffees and teas, the morning fare includes pastries, bagels, waffles, and fruit smoothies, while midday, there's a range of grilled sandwiches, from avocado, Brie, and red onion to grilled chicken with roasted red pepper and mango. Vegetarians have several options, including the Sumzie salad—a mountain of greens, veggies, dried fruit, and nuts. In July and August, they're open for dinner and often feature live music. Service can be leisurely, so don't dash in if you're rushing to catch the ferry.

Several places in Tobermory serve fish 'n' chips, but you can't miss the bright blue and yellow facade of **The Fish and Chip Place** (24 Bay St. S., 519/596-8380, www.thefishand-chipplace.com, open late May–mid-Oct. with seasonal hours, $7–12). The small menu includes the eponymous whitefish and French fries; their fish taco won't put any Baja joints out of business, but this far north of the border, it will do. On a sunny afternoon, particularly if you've been hiking, a beer on their deck is a perfect reward.

Information and Services

The **Tobermory Chamber of Commerce Information Centre** (Hwy. 6, just south of Little Tub Harbour, 519/596-2452, www.tobermory.org) can provide maps and information about attractions, lodging, and services. You can also park your car here for the day at no charge. **County of Bruce Tourism** (www.explorethebruce.com) has extensive information about Tobermory and the rest of the Bruce Peninsula.

The **Foodland Market** (9 Bay St., 519/596-2380, 7 A.M.–9 P.M. daily) at Little Tub Harbour stocks basic supplies for picnics or camping and also has a laundromat.

Getting There and Around

Tobermory is approximately 300 kilometers (186 miles) northwest of Toronto. It's about a four-hour drive, weather and traffic permitting. Parking around Little Tub Harbour is restricted to two hours. If you're planning a longer stay in town, or heading out on a boat tour, leave your car in one of the free long-term parking lots. There's one at the Tobermory Chamber of Commerce Information Centre on Highway 6, two smaller lots on Head Street (between the Information Centre and Little Tub Harbour), and another on Legion Street, west of Highway 6.

Without a car, you can easily walk around Tobermory or to the National Park Visitor Centre, catch a boat to Flowerpot Island, and take other short hikes in the area. Some hotel or B&B owners will drop you at the trailhead for a day hike, so inquire when making lodging reservations. **Thorncrest Outfitters** (7441 Hwy. 6, 519/596-8908, www.thorncrestoutfitters.com) runs a shuttle service for hikers or paddlers (they'll also transport your canoe or kayak) between Tobermory and Cyprus Lake, Dyer's Bay, or Lion's Head.

While there's no direct bus service to Tobermory, you can connect through Owen Sound. **First Student Canada bus service** (2180 20th St. E., Owen Sound, 519/376-5712, one-way adults $28, children 12 and under $14) runs one bus a day in each direction between Owen Sound and Tobermory on Fridays, Saturdays, Sundays, and holiday Mondays from July through early September. The schedule is timed to connect with the Manitoulin Island ferry. **Greyhound Bus Lines** (800/661-8747, www.greyhound.ca) can get you to Owen Sound from Toronto and from points farther afield.

The **M.S. Chi-Cheemaun Ferry** (519/376-6601 information, 800/265-3163 reservations, www.ontarioferries.com), nicknamed "The Big Canoe," runs mid-May to mid-October between Tobermory and South Baymouth on Manitoulin Island. The crossing takes about two hours, and the ship accommodates 638 passengers and 143 cars. The ferry cuts out several hours of driving time, compared to the road route between Southern Ontario and Manitoulin. Reservations are recommended, particularly if you're taking a car. The Tobermory ferry terminal is at 8 Eliza Street (519/596-2510).

◖ BRUCE PENINSULA NATIONAL PARK

Intricate rock formations. Caribbean-blue water. Centuries-old trees. Inland lakes. More than three dozen types of orchids. The Bruce Peninsula National Park (www.pc.gc.ca, open year-round, $11.70/vehicle), which encompasses 156 square kilometers (60 square miles) spread out over several parcels of land, protects these natural features that are unique in Ontario. The park is at the northern tip of the Bruce Peninsula near the town of Tobermory.

The Grotto and Indian Head Cove

The park's most visited sights are the Grotto, a

waterside cave, and the adjacent Indian Head Cove. And with good reason. Through centuries of erosion, the waters of Georgian Bay have sculpted the area's soft limestone cliffs, leaving dramatic overhangs, carved rocks, and underwater caves, such as the Grotto. At Indian Head Cove, the rocks are sculpted into pillars, narrower at the bottom and wider at the top, resembling smaller versions of the "flowerpots" in the Fathom Five National Marine Park. Particularly on bright sunny days, the contrast between the brilliant blue-green bay, the polished white rocks along the shoreline, and the layered rock cliffs is striking.

You can climb down to sea level to explore the cave-like Grotto, but even if scrambling down steep rocks isn't your thing, you can still view the Grotto from above. At Indian Head Cove, the rock formations are on the pebbly beach, so no climbing is required. You can swim in Georgian Bay here, although the water is cold year-round.

It's a moderate hike to the Grotto from the day-use parking area near the **Cyprus Lake Park Office** (Cyprus Lake Rd., off Highway 6, 519/596-2263), where several trails lead to Georgian Bay. Once at the shore, head north along the rocky shore to Indian Head Cove and then to the Grotto. Allow about 30–45 minutes to walk each way from the parking area. You must stop at the park office to pay a day-use parking fee ($11.70 per car) before you set out. There are restrooms at the Cyprus Lake office and near the Grotto, but no other services, so bring whatever food and water you need.

Cyprus Lake

From the Cyprus Lake day-use parking area (Cyprus Lake Rd., off Highway 6), you can walk down to the lake itself in just a few minutes. There's a sandy beach with somewhat warmer water than in chilly Georgian Bay, as well as picnic tables.

The **Cyprus Lake Trail** follows the lakeshore. A mostly flat, 5.2-kilometer (3.2-mile) loop trail, it's a popular spot for bird-watching. Paddlers looking for a calm body of

water to canoe or kayak can head out into Cyprus Lake. In winter, you can snowshoe along Cyprus Lake and on to the Grotto. Park at the Cyprus Lake main gate, then follow the Cyprus Lake Trail to the Georgian Bay Trail.

There are no boat rentals at the lake, but in Tobermory, **Thorncrest Outfitters** (7441 Hwy. 6, 519/596-8908, www.thorncrestoutfitters.com) rents canoes and kayaks and can transport them to the lake. They also offer a number of full- and half-day guided paddling trips at various locations on the northern Bruce Peninsula and rent snowshoes ($15/day) in winter.

◖ The Bruce Trail

Serious hikers often plan their holidays to hike the Bruce Trail (www.brucetrail.org), doing sections of this 845-kilometer (525-mile) route in two-day, three-day, or week-long increments. They return to the trail until they've completed the entire route from the Niagara region to Tobermory. Yet you don't have to be an indomitable whole-trail hiker to enjoy the Bruce Trail. You can easily take day hikes along the trail, in and around the Bruce Peninsula National Park.

From the Grotto, the Bruce Trail extends along Georgian Bay in both directions. If you continue to the west, you can hike all the way to Tobermory (18 kilometers, or 11 miles). Between the Grotto and Little Cove (12.6 kilometers, or 7.8 miles), the trail is quite difficult, with very rocky terrain, but you're rewarded with sweeping views of Georgian Bay. From Little Cove to Tobermory (5.4 kilometers, or 3.4 miles), the trail flattens out and wends through the cedar forest.

Heading east from the Grotto along the bay, the Bruce Trail hugs the shore to Stormhaven (2.4 kilometers, or 1.5 miles), where there's a primitive camping area and restroom. The trail then gets more difficult for the next 9.5 kilometers (6 miles) to the High Dump camping area.

Because many sections of the Bruce Trail are quite rugged, get details about your route

BRUCE TRAIL
- FOLLOW THE WHITE BLAZES
  - BLUE BLAZES FOR SIDE TRAILS-
- RESPECT THE NATURAL BEAUTY OF
  THE LION'S HEAD NATURE RESERVE.

DESTINATION	DISTANCE (One Way)
LION'S HEAD POTHOLE	400 m
FIRST LOOKOUT	600 m
LION'S HEAD LOOKOUT	1.3 km
MCKAY'S HARBOUR	3.6 km

© CAROLYN B. HELLER

The Bruce Trail runs from the Niagara region to the Bruce Peninsula.

before you set out. The staff at the Cyprus Lake Park Office or the National Park Visitor Centre can help match a hike to your ability level.

Singing Sands Beach

On the west side of the peninsula, Singing Sands Beach (Dorcas Bay Rd.) looks like it's part of a completely different natural environment than the rocky eastern shores—and it is. The flat, sandy beach spreads out around Dorcas Bay with vistas out across Lake Huron; it's a popular swimming spot. A short boardwalk trail loops around an adjacent marsh, and the three-kilometer (1.9-mile) **Forest Beach Loop Trail** is another easy walk that's good for bird-watching.

Camping

Within Bruce Peninsula National Park, the **Cyprus Lake Campground** (Cyprus Lake Rd., $23.40 mid-Apr.–mid-Oct., $15.70 mid-Oct.–Apr.) has 242 drive-in campsites

in three camping areas. All three areas border Cyprus Lake and have restroom facilities with flush toilets and cold-water taps, but no showers. No electrical or sewer hookups are available. There are showers at Little Tub Harbour in Tobermory, about 15 kilometers (9 miles) north of Cyprus Lake. The campground is open year-round. Between May and mid-October, you can reserve campsites through the Parks Canada Campground Reservation Service (877/737-3783, www.pccamping.ca). Reservations are recommended, particularly during July and August. Reservations aren't taken between mid-October and April, when sites are first-come, first-served.

Also in the park are two primitive backcountry campgrounds ($9.80/person): **Stormhaven** and **High Dump**. Stormhaven is 2.4 kilometers (1.5 miles) east of the Grotto along Georgian Bay. High Dump is 9.5 kilometers (6 miles) east of Stormhaven, or eight kilometers (five miles) from the parking area at Crane Lake

THE BRUCE TRAIL

One of Canada's iconic outdoor experiences is a hike along Ontario's Bruce Trail, an 845-kilometer (525-mile) hiking route that extends from the Niagara region to the tip of the Bruce Peninsula. How long does it take to complete the whole trail? If you hiked eight hours a day, covering about 30 kilometers (19 miles), it would take you roughly a month to hike "end to end." However, unless you're an experienced hiker, this pace will likely be much too fast. And while some hikers do the entire trail straight through, far more "end to end" hikers complete the trail in a series of shorter excursions over several months or years.

Some sections of the trail are flat and easy, while others are quite rugged– get information about your route before you set out. A good source of trail information is the **Bruce Trail Conservatory** (905/529-6821 or 800/665-4453, www.brucetrail.org), a charitable organization committed to protecting and promoting the trail. They have a free online overview map, and you can download detailed maps of individual trail sections ($3/map). If you're serious about hiking the entire trail, consider purchasing the **Bruce Trail Reference** ($36.95), available on the conservatory website or through Canadian bookseller Chapters/Indigo (www.chapters.indigo.ca). Many Canadian libraries stock the guide, too. It's updated regularly – and there are changes and additions to the trail– so check for the most recent edition.

If you'd like to find hiking companions or join in group hikes, check out one of the nine Bruce Trail clubs, which help maintain the trail and arrange group activities in different regions. The **Peninsula Bruce Trail Club** (www.pbtc.ca) organizes hikes throughout the year on the Bruce Peninsula and also publishes guides to peninsula day hikes. You can get a list of all the trail clubs from the Bruce Trail Conservatory website (www.brucetrail.org).

The Bruce Trail Conservatory website includes a list of campgrounds that are accessible to the trail, as well as B&Bs and inns that welcome trail hikers. Many innkeepers whose lodgings are close to the trail will pick up or drop off hikers at nearby trailheads.

Another option for hikers who don't want to camp or lug gear is the **Home-to-Home B&B Network** (888/301-3224, www.hometohome-network.ca). Stay at any lodgings in this network of B&Bs, located between Wiarton and Tobermory, and hike to your next destination. The B&B owners will move your luggage to your next lodging, where dinner will be waiting. In the morning, you'll have a hot breakfast before beginning the day's hike. If you want a picnic lunch to eat on the go, that can be arranged, too. A Home-to-Home coordinator will help plan your hiking route and arrange accommodations. Reservations are required at least two weeks in advance.

(from Highway 6, take Dyers Bay Road east to Crane Lake Road). To reach either area, you need to backpack in along the Bruce Trail. You must register at the Cyprus Lake Park Office (Cyprus Lake Rd., off Highway 6) before heading out. Between May and October, you can register by phone (519/596-2263) or in person at the office; the rest of the year, register at the self-service kiosk outside the office.

Stormhaven and High Dump each have nine sites with tent platforms and a composting toilet. No water is available, so bring your own or purify the water from the bay.

If you don't want to camp, the closest accommodations to the national park are in Tobermory.

Information and Services
For general information about the Bruce Peninsula National Park, phone or visit the **National Park Visitor Centre** (120 Chi Sin Tib Dek Rd., Tobermory, 519/596-2233, www.pc.gc.ca). Between May and October, you can also contact the **Cyprus Lake Park Office** (Cyprus Lake Rd., off Highway 6, 519/596-2263).

◖ FATHOM FIVE NATIONAL MARINE PARK

One of only three national marine conservation areas in Canada, Fathom Five National Marine Park (519/596-2233, www.pc.gc.ca) includes 22 islands in Georgian Bay off the northern end of the Bruce Peninsula. Access to the park is by boat from the town of Tobermory. Formed over 400 million years ago, these rocky islands are composed primarily of dolomite, a type of limestone. The main attractions for visitors are the distinctive rock formations are known as "flowerpots." Narrow at the bottom and wider at the top, these rock stacks resemble massive stone pots. While the waves have slowly worn away the softer limestone on the pillars' lower end, the harder dolomite tops have survived, creating the unusual shape.

More than 20 shipwrecks lie within the Fathom Five park's territory, making it a popular destination for scuba divers. In fact, the park gets its name from William Shakespeare's play *The Tempest,* in which the following lines describe the father of Ferdinand, who is feared dead in a shipwreck:

Full fathom five thy father lies;
Of his bones are coral made;
Those are pearls that were his eyes:
Nothing of him that doth fade
But doth suffer a sea-change
Into something rich and strange.
Sea-nymphs hourly ring his knell
Hark! now I hear them, ding-dong, bell.

A "fathom" is a unit of measure roughly equal to 1.8 meters, or six feet, so "fathom five" is nine meters, or about 30 feet. A long way down!

Scuba Diving

While you might not think of such a northern location as a prime scuba destination, Fathom Five has some of the world's best freshwater diving. Not only is the water generally clear, but the combination of underwater cliffs, caves, and other geological formations, along with the more than 20 shipwrecks in the area, give divers plenty to explore.

All divers must register in person at the National Park Visitor Centre in Tobermory (120 Chi Sin Tib Dek Rd., 519/596-2233, www.pc.gc.ca, adults $5.80, seniors $4.90, children $2.90). The park charges divers a per-person daily fee of $4.90 in addition to the park admission fee and the cost of boat transport. If you're planning to dive at least four days, buy an annual divers' pass for $19.60. Several companies in Tobermory run single-day and multiday dive trips to the Fathom Five islands and surrounding areas. They also offer scuba lessons and gear rentals. Contact **Divers Den** (3 Bay St., 519/596-2363, www.diversden.ca), **G+S Watersports** (8 Bay St. South, 519/596-2200, www.gswatersports.net), or **Tobermory Aquasports** (7037 Hwy. 6, 519/596-8474, www.tobermoryaquasports.com).

Flowerpot Island

Unless you have your own boat, only one of the park's 22 islands is accessible to visitors: Flowerpot Island, named for the two towering

one of the "flowerpots" in the Fathom Five National Marine Park

© CAROLYN B. HELLER

rock pillars known as the "flowerpots." These rock stacks sit waterside on the island's eastern shore.

Tour boats from Tobermory dock at Beachy Cove on the east side of Flowerpot Island. The island isn't large (about 2 square kilometers, or 0.77 square mile), so it's only about a 15-minute walk from Beachy Cove to the first **small flowerpot** (which is 7 meters, or 23 feet, high), and a few minutes farther to the **large flowerpot,** which stands 12 meters (40 feet) tall. From the flowerpots, you can follow the **Loop Trail,** passing a small cave. (The path up to the cave is easy to miss; it's on the left just beyond the flowerpots.) You can't go inside the cave, but you can peer into the entrance.

Beyond the cave, the Loop Trail continues to the **Flowerpot Island Lightstation** on the island's northeast tip. The first lighthouse on the island went into service in 1897; in the 1960s, the original light was replaced with a steel lighthouse tower that's still flashing its beacon today. You can walk out to the tower and to an adjacent observation deck with a view across Georgian Bay. Near the lightstation is the lightkeeper's house, which contains a small museum (July–Aug.).

To return to Beachy Cove from the lighthouse, either backtrack along the trail past the flowerpots or continue on the Loop Trail up and over the bluffs in the middle of the island. This latter section of the Loop Trail is much more rugged; park staff advise allowing at least an extra hour to return via this route.

If you can tolerate cold water, you can swim or snorkel off Flowerpot Island. The beaches are rocky, so you might want to wear protective footwear. The best spots to swim are near Beachy Cove (either near the picnic shelter or the campground) or around the flowerpots. In either location, be alert for boat traffic.

CAMPING

Camping is your only option if you want to spend the night on Flowerpot Island. The park accepts camping reservations (519/596-2233, ext. 221) each year beginning in early May. The **Flowerpot Island Campground** ($9.80/

person) has six basic tent sites, all a stone's throw from the shore and a 5–10-minute walk from the Beachy Cove boat dock. There's a composting toilet nearby but no showers or running water. You need to bring your own water or purify the bay water for drinking.

No supplies are available on the island, so bring food and anything else you might need. Parks Canada cautions that campers should bring enough food, water, and warm clothing to last extra days, since the boat service back to the mainland can be canceled if the weather turns bad.

INFORMATION AND SERVICES

Park staff are frequently on duty at Flowerpot Island's Beachy Cove during the summer months. Otherwise, staff may or may not be available on the island, so if you have questions, check at the visitor center (120 Chi Sin Tib Dek Rd., 519/596-2233, www.pc.gc.ca, adults $5.80, seniors $4.90, children $2.90) before you leave Tobermory.

A small volunteer-run snack bar near the lighthouse is open during the summer, but hours are erratic; be sure to bring water and snacks with you. There are restrooms at Beachy Cove between the ferry dock and the campground, as well as near the lighthouse. It's almost worth hiking to the lightstation just to use the "Loo with a View," with its vistas across the bay.

GETTING THERE

The park service does not run its own boats; instead, it works with a private company, **Blue Heron Tours** (Little Tub Harbour, 519/596-2999, www.blueheronco.com, mid-May–mid-Oct.) that offers several types of boat trips to Flowerpot Island. The sailing schedules vary seasonally, so check their website or phone for details. Also confirm when the last boats leave Flowerpot Island to return to the mainland, and get back to the dock at Beachy Cove in plenty of time. You don't want an unexpected overnight stay!

If you just want to get to Flowerpot Island, take Blue Heron's 15-minute direct shuttle boat (adults $33.19, seniors $31.42, children

4–12 $24.34 round-trip) between Little Tub Harbour and Beachy Cove. Boats drop off and pick up passengers several times a day.

For a few dollars more, you can add a brief ride through Big Tub Harbour to look at the remains of two shipwrecks on the 25-minute island shuttle and shipwrecks tour (adults $37.62, seniors $35.85, children 4–12 $28.77 round-trip). You don't see much—the wrecks look like shadows under the water—but it's as close as you can get to the sunken ships without scuba diving.

On the one-hour *Blue Heron V* glass bottom boat tour (with Flowerpot Island: adults $37.62, seniors $35.85, kids 4–12 $28.77; boat tour only: adults $28.77, seniors $26.99, kids 4–12 $19.92) you can visit the Big Tub shipwrecks and cruise around Flowerpot Island with an option to disembark on the island.

You must pay the national park admission fee (adults $5.80, seniors $4.90, children $2.90) in addition to the price for the boat trips. Park admission includes access to the National Park Visitor Centre in Tobermory, as well as admission to Flowerpot Island.

DYER'S BAY

Unlike many of the Bruce Peninsula's lighthouses, which you can see only from the exterior, at the **Cabot Head Lighthouse** (www.cabothead.ca, 10 A.M.–7 P.M. daily late May–mid-Oct., suggested donation $3), you can venture inside. The lower levels of the red-and-white wooden structure are a museum with exhibits about local marine history. You can climb up to the observation tower for a lightkeeper's-eye-view out across the bay. The original Cabot Head Lighthouse began operation in 1896. It remained in use until 1968, when it was torn down and replaced with the current light, which is an automated beacon.

The lighthouse is about 40 kilometers (25 miles) southeast of Tobermory, about a 45–50-minute drive. From Highway 6, go east on Dyer's Bay Road. Once you pass through the village of Dyer's Bay, the road becomes a winding gravel track that twists along the shoreline to the lighthouse.

LION'S HEAD

Lion's Head is a friendly little village on Georgian Bay in the approximate north–south midpoint of the Bruce Peninsula. With its central location, it's a convenient base for exploring the peninsula, particularly if you want to visit sights beyond the Tobermory area. And if you want to stay put, you can stroll or swim at the beach, browse in the village shops, or have a beer in the local pub. Set on the bay at the mouth of Lion's Head harbor, **Lion's Head Lighthouse** is a re-creation of the original lightstation built here in 1903. Students at the local high school constructed the current lighthouse in 1983, using plans for the original structure. The lighthouse is particularly photogenic, perched on the shore with the bay and the cliffs of the Niagara Escarpment behind.

On the south side of town, **Lion's Head Provincial Park** (519/389-9056, www.ontarioparks.com, free) is known for its "potholes," deep, cylindrical holes carved by erosion into the limestone rocks. It's about a 15–20-minute walk along a flat section of the Bruce Trail to two of the large potholes. The trail continues toward Georgian Bay, where it becomes much more difficult as it hugs the cliffs. The reward for the climb up and along the tops of the rocks is a spectacular view of the cliffs and the bay. This section of the trail isn't recommended for small children, as the trail veers quite close to the cliffs. Access to the potholes trail is from Moore Street. Don't be deterred by the "No Exit" sign on Moore Street; it just means that the road dead-ends. The trail starts opposite 128 Moore Street. The park has no restrooms or other services.

The **Central Bruce Peninsula Chamber Of Commerce** (519/793-3178, www.central-brucepeninsula.ca, daily July–Aug., Sat.–Sun. mid-May–June and Sept.–mid-Oct.) runs a seasonal tourist information center on Highway 6 in Ferndale, at the intersection of Highway 9 (the Lion's Head turnoff). The rest of the year, staff answer questions by phone. Lion's Head is about 250 kilometers (160 miles) north of Toronto, and there's no public transportation to or around the area.

Accommodations and Food

Big rooms, a beachside location, and a warm welcome are the reasons to stay at the **Lion's Head Beach Motel and Cottages** (1 McNeil St., 519/793-3155, www.lionsheadbeachmotelandcottages.ca, $95–105 s, $109–119 d). Although the motel rooms won't win any design prizes, they're well maintained and larger than average, and they include kitchenettes. They're spacious enough to accommodate a family, but the newer two- and three-bedroom cottages would be even more comfortable if you've brought Grandma or the kids.

If you're not a regular at **The Lion's Head Inn & Restaurant** (8 Helen St., 519/793-4601, www.lionsheadinn.ca, lunch and dinner daily May–Oct., Wed.–Sat. Nov.–Apr., $10–20), you may feel like one after you've dined in this convivial restaurant and pub. The food is a notch above your basic pub fare, starting with burgers and pasta and moving on to grilled whitefish, steak, even chicken Cordon Bleu. The best value is the Friday all-you-can-eat fish 'n' chips special ($15); you need a hearty appetite to tackle more than three pieces of fish, but the last I heard, the fish-eating record was 11! Built as a boardinghouse in 1879, the inn also has three simple guest rooms upstairs ($65 d with shared bath, $80 d with private bath).

It's worth visiting the small **Lion's Head Farmers' Market** (9 A.M.–noon Sat. late May–mid-Oct.) just for its open-air setting right on Lion's Head Beach. Vendors sell produce, muffins, and other baked goods, as well as crafts.

Perfect for a country getaway, hiker's respite, or a plentiful farm-style supper, the **❰ Cape Chin Connection Country Inn** (418 Cape Chin North Rd., 519/795-7525, www.capechin.ca, $70s, $90 d with shared bath, $105 s or d with private bath, open year-round) is set on a 40-hectare (100-acre) homestead about 25 kilometers (16 miles) north of Lion's Head Village. Although additions have been made over the years, the original 1853 log farmhouse remains and now contains one of the dining rooms. On the main floor, there's one guest room with private bath; upstairs, the five smallish bedrooms, with floral wallpaper and

country quilts, share two bathrooms. Room rates include a full breakfast, and packages including breakfast, a packed lunch, and a five-course dinner are also available. Nonguests are welcome in the restaurant for the five-course prix-fixe dinners (6–9 P.M. daily, $27–33) by reservation; the beer-braised pork ribs are a favorite among the hearty homestyle dishes. Owners Ann and Don Bard, who've run the inn since 1988, can tell you pretty much anything you need to know about the region; they were founding members of the Home-to-Home B&B network, which provides lodging and meals to Bruce Trail hikers (the Bruce Trail crosses the inn's property).

Craving butter tarts, hearty potato-filled "pasties," or homemade multigrain bread? Then pull off Highway 6 at the **Harvest Moon Organic Bakery** (3927 Hwy. 6, 519/592-5742, www.harvestmoonbakery.ca, 9 A.M.–4:30 P.M. Wed.–Sun. July–Aug., Thurs.–Sun. May–June and Sept.–Oct.). Besides sampling the treats that come out of this riotously colorful little house, you can stroll around the quirky sculpture garden (free). The bakery is about 10 minutes north of Ferndale, on the west side of Highway 6.

WIARTON AND VICINITY

The town of Wiarton sits on Colpoys Bay, an inlet off of Georgian Bay, with the cliffs of the Niagara Escarpment towering above the water. Highway 6, the peninsula's main north–south route, runs straight through town, where it's called Berford Street. While it's not a big city (the year-round population is under 2,500), Wiarton does have all the basic services you need, including a 24-hour grocery store. Many of Wiarton's limestone or brick buildings downtown date to the mid-1800s; the village was incorporated in 1880, and the railway reached the area the following year. The former railway station is now the town's information center. Two fingers of land jutting into Georgian Bay on either side of Wiarton are worth exploring. To the north, Cape Crocker is a First Nations reserve; to the east, you can head toward the village of Big Bay, visiting caves, gardens, and an ice cream shop en route.

Wiarton's most famous resident may be **Wiarton Willie,** a weather-forecasting groundhog. Similar to the American "Punxsutawney Phil," Wiarton Willie comes out of his burrow annually on Groundhog Day (Feb. 2). If he sees his shadow, Canada's winter will last for another six weeks; if he doesn't, spring is supposedly on the way. Between May and September, and again in early February, you can view "Willie" in his pen outside the Wiarton branch of the Bruce County Public Library (578 Brown St., at William St.). Local sculptor Dave Robinson crafted a 4.5-ton limestone statue of the town's notable groundhog. *"Willie Emerging"* sits near the beach in **Bluewater Park** (William St.). Also in the park is Wiarton's former train station, an ornate wooden building built in 1904 and moved to its present site in 1971.

East of Wiarton, in the hamlet of Big Bay, you can stroll among the irises, lilacs, poppies, and lavender in the peaceful, privately owned **Kepplecroft Gardens** (504156 Grey Rd. 1, Big Bay, 519/534-1090, www.keppelcroft.com, 10 A.M.–5 P.M. Wed.–Sun. May–mid-Oct., suggested donated $3). Walking paths wend through the property, which includes a Zen garden, a woodland garden, and rock sculptures. The Kepplecroft Gardens are part of a regional network of private gardens, known as the **Rural Gardens of Grey and Bruce Counties** (www.ruralgardens.ca), that are open to visitors. The website lists gardens hours and locations; you can also pick up a "Rural Gardens" map at any of the information centers on the Bruce Peninsula.

Wiarton celebrates its weather-forecasting groundhog during the annual **Wiarton Willie Festival** (519/534-5492, www.wiartonwillie.com), a winter carnival that includes a parade, fireworks, concerts, pancake breakfasts, sleigh rides, and, of course, Willie's prediction for the end of winter. The festival takes place for several days around Groundhog Day (February 2). Get an event schedule on the festival website or from the local tourism offices.

Stop into the **Wiarton Information Centre** (Bluewater Park, 519/534-3111 or 519/534-2592, www.wiartonchamber.ca, May–early

Sept.), run by the local Chamber of Commerce in the former train station. You can also get visitor information from the **Town of South Bruce Peninsula** (315 George St., 519/534-1400 or 877/534-1400, www.southbrucepeninsula.com, 8:30 A.M.–4:30 P.M. Mon.–Fri.), or call the main office for the **County of Bruce Tourism** (578 Brown St., 519/534-5344 or 800/268-3838, www.explorethebruce.com), located in Wiarton. Wiarton is about 220 kilometers (137 miles) northwest of Toronto. There's no public transportation in the area, and it's difficult to explore without a car.

Cape Croker

Part of the Saugeen Ojibway First Nations Territory, the 6,000-hectare (14,825-acre) Cape Croker Peninsula juts out into Georgian Bay north of Wiarton. The peninsula's Ojibway name, *Neyaashiinigmiing,* means "a point of land nearly surrounded by water," and the name is apt—except for a sliver of land connecting the peninsula to the mainland, it's ringed by the waters of the bay. Cape Croker is a pretty spot for a drive or hike, particularly on the north side of the peninsula with views across the water to the limestone bluffs of the Niagara Escarpment. You can drive out to the **Cape Croker Lighthouse,** built in 1902 on the tip of the cape, but the interior isn't open to the public, and the setting behind a chain-link fence isn't that picturesque.

The waters off Cape Croker are popular with kayakers. **Suntrail Source For Adventure** (60 Queen St. E. aka Hwy. 6, Hepworth, 519/935-2478 or 877/882-2958, www.suntrail.net) offers full-day kayak excursions ($99 per person) on Sydney Bay, departing from the Cape Croker Indian Park. They rent kayaks and offer a delivery service, as well. Near the mainland end of the peninsula, the **Cape Croker Indian Park** (519/534-0571, www.capecrokerpark.com, $10/vehicle) has a lovely beach and hiking trails, as well as a campground.

To experience the music, dance, and other traditions of the local First Nations community, visit the Bruce Peninsula during the **Cape Croker Powwow** (www.nawash.ca, late Aug.,

$7), held at Cape Croker Indian Park (519/534-0571, www.capecrokerpark.com, $10/vehicle). Visitors are welcome as long as they are respectful of local customs. Ask permission before taking photos or videos, and leave the beer at home—the powwow is an alcohol-free event.

Accommodations and Food

In the late 1990s, Evan LeBlanc and Dave Peebles bought a basic roadside motel overlooking Colpoys Bay just east of Wiarton, and they've been steadily upgrading the property that is now the three-story **Waterview on the Bay** (501205 Island View Dr., 519/534-0921 or 877/534-0921, www.waterview.ca, Apr.–Dec., $95–155 d). The rooms range from simple motel style with two double beds and a fridge to more deluxe; the nicest are the "luxury suites," with whirlpool tubs, sleigh beds, and expansive bay views. There's a swimming pool out back, and it's a short stroll down to the sandy beach, where complimentary kayaks and paddleboats are available. In summer, an all-you-can-eat breakfast buffet is served daily ($10). The Waterview is family-friendly, pet-friendly, and just overall friendly.

While many people dream of abandoning the city for a simpler rural life, Bonnie Howe and Phil Howard actually made the move when they purchased a farm east of Wiarton and opened the **Longlane Bed & Breakfast** (483078 Colpoy's Range Rd., 519/534-3901, www.longlane.ca, $80 s, $100 d). They raise cattle and chickens (guests can help gather eggs) and grow an expanding array of organic vegetables. Upstairs in the 1902 farmhouse, the three guest rooms are decorated with quilts and country curtains; on the walls are black-and-white photos of the family who originally established the farm. Guests share two bathrooms, as well as a sitting area with a TV, and in the morning, they tuck into hearty farm breakfasts around the communal kitchen table. The owners will shuttle hikers to the Bruce Trail nearby.

Wiarton's best restaurant, the **Green Door Café** (563 Berford St., 510/534-3278, www.thegreendoorcafe.com, contact for seasonal hours) looks like a small-town coffee shop, where local retirees stop in for coffee and grilled cheese sandwiches. At this unassuming eatery, though, the straightforward sandwiches ($5–10) and hearty main dishes ($11–14) are well prepared from fresh ingredients. Try the delicious, garlicky Caesar salad or the meaty cabbage rolls.

The tiny **Big Bay General Store** (Big Bay Sideroad at Grey Rd. 1, 519/534-4523, daily late May–early Sept., Sat.–Sun. only spring and fall), east of Wiarton, doesn't stock many groceries, but if you're looking for delicious homemade ice cream, this is the place. They make more than 80 different flavors, with 10 to 12 available at a time. Call to confirm their hours before making a special trip.

CAMPING

Owned and operated by the Chippewas of Nawash First Nation, the **Cape Croker Indian Park** (519/534-0571, www.capecrokerpark.com, early May–mid-Oct., $25–31 per site) has an enviable waterfront location on Sydney Bay. The 210-hectare (520-acre) property has 315 campsites, with showers, flush toilets, laundry facilities, a swimming beach, and canoe rentals. Prime waterfront sites look across to the cliffs of the Niagara Escarpment, while other sites are tucked into the woods. A small camping cabin with two bunks ($65) is also available. Reservations aren't required, but you may want to book ahead for the popular waterfront sites, for the cabin, or for holiday weekend stays; definitely reserve in advance for the August powwow.

SAUBLE BEACH

On the shore of Lake Huron at the south end of the Bruce Peninsula, Sauble Beach is a full-fledged beach-holiday town. This sun-and-fun community has burger stands and soft-serve ice cream shops, T-shirt sellers and bikini boutiques, and, oh, yes, a sandy lakeshore beach that seems to go on and on.

The world's second-longest freshwater beach, Sauble Beach (Lakeshore Dr.) is a flat paradise of sand that extends for 11 kilometers (nearly seven miles); only Wasaga Beach, east of Collingwood, is longer. The early French explorers who traversed this area named it "La Rivière au Sable" ("River to the Sand") for the nearby Sauble River, but by the end of the 19th-century, the town was known as Sauble Beach for its major geographical asset. Since the water is fairly shallow, Sauble Beach is a good choice for families with younger kids. The atmosphere in July and August can be rather honky-tonk, but the farther you go from the heart of town, the easier it is to find a peaceful spot to lay your towel. And despite the summer crowds, the beach is undeniably beautiful, and sunsets over the lake can be spectacular. Outside summer high season, you'll sometimes have the fine golden sand almost to yourself. Beach parking ($3/hour or $15/day in season) is available in lots right on the sand and along Lakeshore Road. Prepare for epic summer traffic jams. The **Sauble Beach Sandfest** (Lakeshore Blvd., 519/422-2457) takes place the first weekend in August and turns the beach into a giant outdoor sand sculpture gallery, drawing both professional and amateur sand sculptors.

Sauble Beach has a large assortment of standard beach motels and cottages. The **Sauble Beach Information Centre** (672 Main St., 519/422-1262, www.saublebeach.com, call for hours) has information about cottage rentals and lists of area accommodations. If you prefer a more peaceful atmosphere, you could stay in Wiarton (about 20 kilometers, or 12.5 miles, from Sauble Beach) and come to the beach during the day. Restaurants in town tend to serve burgers, pizza, and other eat-and-run fare. Eateries are clustered along Main Street and on Second Avenue North (one block east of the beach).

Sauble Beach is about 220 kilometers (137 miles) northwest of Toronto via Highways 6/10. After you pass through Owen Sound, continue on Highway 6 to Bruce Road 8, which heads west into Sauble Beach.

Sauble Falls Provincial Park

About one kilometer (0.6 mile) north of Sauble Beach, this small provincial park (Sauble Falls Parkway/County Rd. 13, 519/422-1952, www.

ontarioparks.com, late Apr.–Oct., $10–13/vehicle) couldn't feel more different than the frenzied tourist crush of the nearby town. Although it does get busy in summer, it still feels more like an escape into the woods.

The petite waterfalls along the Sauble River that give the park its name descend in tiers, almost like an aquatic wedding cake, over a staircase of dolomite limestone. You can watch the falls from a small viewing platform or along either side of the river; it's a lovely spot for a picnic. In spring and fall, you may see salmon and rainbow trout attempting to swim upstream over each ledge of the falls. You can also go canoeing or kayaking on a stretch of the Sauble River that winds through the park. Canoe and kayak rentals (daily mid-June–early Sept., weekends only early Sept–mid-Oct., call for fall hours) are available off Sauble Falls Parkway just north of the river.

Sauble Falls Provincial Park has 152 campsites ($36.75 tent sites, $42.25 electrical sites). In both the East Campground and the larger, radio-free West Campground, the nicest sites front the Sauble River. Both areas have flush toilets and showers; the West Campground has laundry facilities. You can reserve a campsite up to five months in advance though the Ontario Parks Reservations Service (888/668-7275, www.ontarioparks.com, reservation fees $8.50 for online, $9.50 by phone).

OWEN SOUND

It's hard to imagine that this small community of about 22,000 was once known as "Chicago of the North." From 1885 through 1912, when the Canadian Pacific Railway (CPR) made Owen Sound the terminus of its steamship line, the town's port was the busiest in the upper Great Lakes. Many of the town's Victorian homes and buildings date to this era. Alas, in 1912, the Canadian Pacific Railway moved its shipping operations farther east to Port McNicoll, Ontario, which had better rail connections, thus ending Owen Sound's glory years.

If you're more of a city person than the outdoors type, you could use Owen Sound as a base for exploring the peninsula's sights. From

Owen Sound, it's about a 45-minute drive to Wiarton and 75–90 minutes to Tobermory.

For a small city, Owen Sound has a large number of museums and historic attractions. To stroll through the town's history, pick up the *Historic Downtown Walking Tour* brochure at the **Owen Sound Tourist Information Centre** (1155 First Ave. W., 519/371-9833, www.owensoundtourism.com). Many of the community's grand historic homes, built in the late 1800s, are along First Avenue West, while many Victorian-era commercial buildings still stand along Second Avenue East. To learn about Owen Sound's Afro-Canadian heritage, follow two self-guided tours of sites that were important to the African-Canadian community. Pick up brochures about these tours—*The Freedom Trail,* a 10-kilometer (six-mile) walking or cycling tour, and the *Owen Sound Underground Railroad Driving Tour*—at the Owen Sound Tourist Information Centre (1155 First Ave. W., 519/371-9833, www.owensoundtourism.com) or get details online from the City of Owen Sound's Black History website (www.osblackhistory.com).

Grey Roots Museum and Archives

If you think that a museum about a region's roots is a musty trove of papers and old tools, think again. This contemporary museum (102599 Grey Rd. 18, 519/376-3690 or 877/473-9766, www.greyroots.com, 10 A.M.–5 P.M. daily late May–mid-Oct., 10 A.M.–5 P.M. Tues.–Sat. mid-Oct.–late May) showcases the history and culture of Owen Sound and the surrounding region with cool multimedia features that include films, radio stories, and computer-based displays.

Start in the Grey County gallery, where the permanent "Grey Roots" exhibit introduces you to the people who settled the region—from the local First Nations to early pioneers to notable citizens such as Agnes Macphail, a Grey County native who became Canada's first female member of Parliament. Other galleries host temporary and traveling exhibitions; recent exhibits have focused on First Nations storytelling, Victorian-era death and mourning

customs, and the history of Grey County's African-Canadian population.

If you have kids in tow, explore the **Moreston Heritage Village** (10 A.M.–5 P.M. daily June–early Sept.), a pioneer village on the site that's staffed by costumed volunteers. Watch the blacksmith at work, visit the 1850s log cabin, or check out the schoolhouse.

Museum admission rates vary seasonally. From late May to early September, adults are $8, seniors $6, children 5–13 $4, and families $20. The rest of the year, adults are $6, seniors $5, children $3.50, and families $18.

The museum is located on the south edge of Owen Sound, about seven kilometers (4.4 miles) south of downtown.

Tom Thomson Art Gallery

Artist Tom Thomson (1877–1917) grew up outside Owen Sound in the town of Leith. A member of Ontario's Group of Seven—notable landscape artists of the early 20th century—Thomson is best known for the paintings he created in Algonquin Park between 1912 and 1917, until his death (reportedly by drowning) in Algonquin's Canoe Lake. The small, modern Tom Thomson Art Gallery (840 First Ave. W., 519/376-1932, www.tomthomson.org, 10 A.M.–5 P.M. Mon.–Sat., noon–5 P.M. Sun. late May–mid-Oct.; call for off-season hours; adults $5, seniors and students $3, kids under 12 free) mounts changing exhibits of work by Thomson and other Ontario artists. On Wednesdays and on the third Sunday of every month, admission is by donation. In July and August, the gallery also hosts both a film series and a series of Wednesday-afternoon concerts.

Billy Bishop Home and Museum

Owen Sound native William Avery Bishop (1894–1956), a fighter pilot with the British Royal Flying Corps, became one of the most decorated Canadians serving in World War I. Bishop's childhood home, in a restored Victorian mansion, is now the Billy Bishop Home and Museum (948 3rd Ave. W., 519/371-0031, www.billybishop.org, 10 A.M.–5 P.M. Mon.–Sat., noon–5 P.M. Sun. late May–early

Sept.; call for off-season hours; adults $5, seniors and students $4, children 3–12 $2) that includes artifacts from Bishop's life and from World Wars I and II, with an emphasis on aviation history. A musical about Bishop's life, *Billy Bishop Goes to War,* premiered in 1978 and is one of Canada's most widely produced plays.

Owen Sound Marine and Rail Museum

Located in Owen Sound's former Canadian National Railway station (the station's waiting room now houses the Owen Sound Tourist Information Centre), the Owen Sound Marine and Rail Museum (1155 First Ave. W., 519/371-3333, www.marinerail.com, 10 A.M.–5 P.M. Mon.–Sat., noon–5 P.M. Sun. late May–early Sept.; call for off-season hours; adults $5, seniors and students $4, children 3–12 $2) commemorates the region's glory days as a ship and rail hub in the late 1800s. There are ship models, trains, and an exhibit about working on the railroad; outside the museum, you can climb on board a restored caboose.

Harrison Park and the Black History Cairn

Owen Sound was one of the northernmost stops on the Underground Railroad, the network of safe houses that protected slaves fleeing from the United States in the 1800s.

The Black History Cairn (www.osblackhistory.com), located in Harrison Park (Second Ave. E.), memorializes the slaves' journey to the north. This outdoor sculpture includes eight tiles inlaid in the ground, incorporating quilt patterns that represented coded messages to escaping slaves—according to legend, the patterns were originally sewn into quilts. One pattern symbolizes the North Star, which guided slaves to freedom; a log cabin symbol indicates a safe house along the Underground Railroad; another is a sailboat, signifying a water crossing. Around the tiles is a stone structure representing the ruins of a church, with windows looking out toward the Sydenham River. According to Bonita Johnson de Matteis, the artist who designed the cairn, newly freed slaves might have looked out similar church windows in Owen Sound as they gave thanks for their freedom. Johnson de Matteis herself is a descendent of a slave who escaped from the United States and settled in Owen Sound.

Harrison Park is located off 2nd Avenue East, south of downtown. Once you arrive in Harrison Park, to find the Black History Cairn, walk north from the parking area near the Harrison Park Inn; the cairn is just past the playground. The park is a lovely spot for a picnic, and it's crisscrossed with trails for hiking, running, and cycling; it also has three playgrounds, as well as canoe rentals.

Entertainment and Shopping

Owen Sound is an arts hub for the surrounding region, with theater, concerts, films, and special events year-round. The historic downtown **Roxy Theatre** (251 9th St. E., 519/371-2833 or 888/446-7699, www.roxytheatre.ca), built in 1912, hosts live theater and musical performances throughout the year.

The first weekend in August, Owen Sound's annual **Emancipation Celebration Festival** (Harrison Park, 2nd Ave. E., www.emancipation.ca) recalls the struggles of the former slaves who traveled the Underground Railroad to freedom in Canada. It began in 1862 and is now the longest continuously running emancipation festival in North America. Events include a speaker's forum, music, and a picnic.

From photography to metalwork to jewelry, the **Owen Sound Artists' Co-op** (279 10th St. E., 519/371-0479, www.osartistsco-op.com, 9:30 A.M.–5:30 P.M. Mon.–Sat. and noon–4 P.M. Sun. July–Aug.) displays and sells the work of its roughly 40 member artists, all from the local area.

Accommodations and Food

Owen Sound has plenty of lodging options, ranging from standard chain motels to Victorian-style bed and breakfasts. Several of the chains are on the east side of town along Highway 6/10; the Owen Sound Tourist Information Centre (www.owensoundtourism.com) has online listings.

The most romantic place to stay in town is the ◖ **Highland Manor** (867 4th Ave. "A" W., 519/372-2699 or 877/372-2699, www.highland-manor.ca, $120 s, $140–160 d, children under 12 not permitted), a grand brick mansion on a shady residential street. On the first floor, the high ceilings, polished wood floors, and marble fireplaces create an elegant feel; guests can browse books about the area in the library, take their elaborate breakfasts in the formal dining room, and sip drinks in the music room (with a 1902 grand piano) or outside on the veranda. Upstairs, the guest rooms are equally refined, with working fireplaces, antique furnishings, and diaphanous drapes. Owners Linda Bradford and Paul Neville are passionate about local history, and they're a wealth of information about things to see and do nearby.

Although it's out of the town center on a charmless stretch of road and most of its 100 rooms are standard chain accommodations, the **Best Western Inn on the Bay** (1800 2nd Ave. E., 519/371-9200 or 800/780-7234, www.bestwesternontario.com, $140–240 d) does have rooms that overlook Georgian Bay. There's no pool, but the hot tub faces the waterfront.

If you'd like to wander and check out food options, head downtown to 2nd Avenue East, between 10th and Seventh Streets. The **Owen Sound Farmers' Market** (114 8th St. E., 519/371-3433, www.owensoundfarmersmarket.ca, 7 A.M.–2:30 P.M. Sat.) sells baked goods, snacks, and crafts in addition to seasonal produce. Located downtown opposite City Hall, the market is open Saturdays year-round.

As its name suggests, the **Ginger Press Bookshop and Café** (848 2nd Ave. E., 519/376-4233, www.gingerpress.com) is part bookstore and part casual café. You can browse or linger over a coffee during regular bookshop hours (9:30 A.M.–6 P.M. Mon.–Fri., 9 A.M.–4 P.M. Sat.). The kitchen is open for soup, sandwiches, and other light meals (9:30 A.M.–2 P.M. Mon.–Fri., 9 A.M.–noon Sat.). Fresh-pressed apple ginger juice is their specialty. Free Wi-Fi.

At the eclectic **Rocky Raccoon Café** (941 2nd Ave. E., 519/374-0500, www.rockyraccooncafe.

com, noon–10 P.M. daily, $15–25), local ingredients join Asian and global influences to create world-beat dishes that ramble from Thai-style venison to elk curry to whitefish with dill-mango tartar sauce. Weekday buffet lunches ($15) typically feature curries from chef-owner Robin Pradhan's native Nepal.

Practicalities

The **Owen Sound Tourist Information Centre** (1155 First Ave. W., 519/371-9833 or 888/675-5555, www.owensoundtourism.com), just north of downtown, shares a building with the Marine and Rail Museum. You can pick up lots of information about attractions and lodgings around town. The regional tourism association, **Grey County Tourism** (102599 Grey Rd. 18, 519/376-3265 or 877/733-4739, www.visitgrey.ca), has a helpful information desk in the lobby of the Grey Roots Museum.

Owen Sound is 190 kilometers (120 miles) northwest of Toronto, about a 2.5-hour drive via Highways 6 and 10. **Greyhound Bus Lines** (City Transit Centre, 1020 3rd Ave. E., 519/376-5375 or 800/661-8747, www.greyhound.ca) runs two direct buses daily in each direction between Toronto and Owen Sound (about four hours, $33–43 per person).

The **Grey Bruce Airbus** (800/361-0393, www.greybruceairbus.com, one-way/round-trip adults $70/125) operates four trips daily in each direction between Toronto's Pearson Airport and the Owen Sound Days Inn (950 6th St. E.).

The majority of Owen Sound's roadways are numbered streets and avenues (streets run east–west, avenues run north–south). The Sydenham River divides the east and west sides, so a "West" address, such as the Tom Thomson Gallery on 1st Avenue West, is west of the river, while an "East" address is the east of the river.

Owen Sound's attractions are clustered in two main areas—around downtown and south of the center. The main downtown shopping street is 2nd Avenue East, south of 10th Street and east of the river. From downtown, you can continue south on 2nd Avenue East to reach Harrison Park and the Grey Roots Museum.

Owen Sound has a walkable downtown core and you can get around town on **Owen Sound Transit** buses (Downtown Transit Terminal, 1020 3rd Ave. E., 519/376-3299, www.owensound.ca, adults $2, students $1.50, kids under 5 free). Buses operate 6:30 A.M.–6 P.M. Monday through Friday and 9 A.M.–5:30 P.M. Saturday. (Note that there's no evening or Sunday service.) One useful route is the Crosstown loop, which circles between downtown and Harrison Park.

To explore the surrounding towns or further up the Bruce Peninsula, it's much easier to have your own wheels. Car rental companies with offices in Owen Sound include: **Enterprise Rent-A-Car** (669 10th St. W., 519/371-9777 or 800/736-8222, www.enterpriserentacar.ca), **Thrifty Car Rental** (2055 16th Ave. E., 519/371-3381 or 800/371-3381, www.thrifty.com), and **Discount Car Rentals** (677 6th St. E., 519/372-0532, www.discountcar.com).

Collingwood and the Blue Mountains

The Blue Mountain Resort, just outside the town of Collingwood, is Ontario's top ski destination. If you're expecting the Alps or the Rockies, you may chuckle when you see the size of the "mountains" here, but these rolling hills should have plenty of terrain to keep most skiers or snowboarders occupied for at least several days. Besides the winter snow-sports season, the busiest times are midsummer (for mountain biking, hiking, golfing, and other outdoor activities) and fall weekends, when the trees are blazing with color.

Collingwood (population 17,000) serves skiers and other outdoor adventurers with grocery stores, movie theaters, and restaurants; it's also a good base for exploring the region. If your goal is skiing, snowboarding, or other outdoor pursuits, it's most convenient to stay in the Village at Blue Mountain, the resort area at the base of the mountain. If you want more options for dining, shopping, or touring, or if you like lodging with more personality, stay in or near Collingwood.

BLUE MOUNTAIN RESORT

Owned by resort giant Intrawest, Blue Mountain (108 Jozo Weider Blvd., 705/445-0231 or 877/445-0231, www.bluemountain.ca) may remind you of other North American ski towns (at least those with a big corporate parent). The village is car-free, and casually upscale restaurants, bars, and outdoor clothing shops line the pedestrian streets. You can easily walk from village lodgings to the lifts, or if you stay in one of the condo developments around the village, a free shuttle will pick you up.

Blue Mountain Activity Central (705/445-5522, www.activitycentral.ca) acts as an activity "concierge" for guests. They keep a schedule of regular events, including free guided hikes or snowshoe tours, sleigh rides, scavenger hunts, toboggan tours, and more, as well as activities for kids and teens. They can also book activities for you, both on and off the mountain.

Blue Mountain's newest attraction is the **Ridge Runner Mountain Coaster** (10 A.M.–8 P.M. late June–early Sept., call for off-season hours; adults and kids 12 and older $15/ride, $24/two rides; kids 3–12 $5/ride), which twists and turns from the top of the Glades area through the trees and down to the village. One or two people can ride together in each car, and the riders control the car's speed. At least one of the riders must be at least 12 years old and 137 centimeters (54 inches) tall.

Still looking for more things to do? Hiking, tennis, golf, miniature golf, indoor rock climbing, and riding the **Blue Mountain Gondola** (late May–mid-Oct., $4–7) are among the many other mountain activities.

Special events take place at Blue Mountain nearly every weekend from July through early October and on select weekends during the rest of the year. Highlights include the **May Long Weekend Music and Fireworks** (late May),

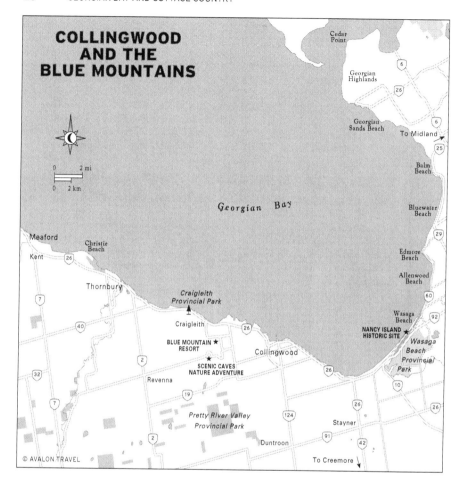

COLLINGWOOD AND THE BLUE MOUNTAINS

Salsa at Blue Mountain (late June), **Village Beach Party** (early Aug.), **Apple Harvest Festival** (early October), and **Oktoberfest at Blue** (late Oct.).

Skiing and Snowboarding

Blue Mountain Resort (108 Jozo Weider Blvd., 705/445-0231 or 877/445-0231, www.bluemountain.ca) began life as a winter sports mecca and now has 15 lifts serving 36 trails. At 720 vertical feet, it's not a tall mountain, nor does it get buried in snow like the western resorts, but an extensive snow-making operation supplements the average annual snowfall of 280 centimeters (110 inches). The winter season typically starts in December and runs through March. Come midweek to avoid the crowds.

Lift tickets (adults $59, seniors and children 6–17 $40) are good for either day skiing (9 A.M.–4:30 P.M.) or afternoon/night skiing (12:30–10 P.M.). If you just want to ski in the evening (4:30–10 P.M.), when 25 of the 36 trails are open, tickets are $40. Ski and

WILD WINTER ADVENTURES

Ontario may not have the towering mountains of western Canada, but that doesn't mean you can't take to the slopes. Not only do the Georgian Bay and Cottage Country regions north of Toronto have several spots for downhill skiing and snowboarding, but there are also plenty of opportunities for cross-country skiing, snowshoeing, dogsledding, and other winter adventures. The Ottawa Valley region, a short drive from the nation's capital, is the other major Ontario destination for winter sports.

The **Blue Mountain Resort** (705/445-0231 or 877/445-0231, www.bluemountain.ca) is the largest downhill ski resort in Ontario and also offers mountain biking and other outdoor sports when the snow season ends. Even closer to Toronto, the **Horseshoe Resort** (1101 Horseshoe Valley Rd., Barrie, 705/835-2790 or 800/461-5627, www.horseshoeresort. com), just north of Barrie off Highway 400, has downhill skiing and snowboarding, golf, even a treetop trekking course.

If you're looking for more places to ski or snowboard, check the **Ontario Snow Resorts Association** (www.skiontario.ca) or make tracks to one of the following mountain resorts:

- **Calabogie Peaks Resort** (30 Barrett Chute Rd., Calabogie, 613/752-2720 or 800/669-4861, www.calabogie.com)

- **Dagmar Ski Resort** (1220 Lakeridge Rd., Ashburn, 905/649-2002, www.skidagmar. com)

- **Hidden Valley Highlands Ski Area** (1655 Hidden Valley Rd., Huntsville, 705/789-1773 or 800/398-9555, www.skihiddenvalley. on.ca)

- **Hockley Valley Ski Resort** (R.R. 1, Orangeville, 519/942-0754, www.hockley.com)

- **Lakeridge** (790 Chalk Lake Rd., Uxbridge, 905/649-2058, www.ski-lakeridge.com)

- **Mount Pakenham** (McWatty Rd., Pakenham, 613/624-5290, www.mountpakenham. com)

- **Mount St. Louis Moonstone** (R.R. 4, Coldwater, 705/835-2112, www.mslm.on.ca)

- **Searchmont Ski Resort** (103 Searchmont Resort Rd., Searchmont, 705/781-2340, www.searchmont.com)

snowboard rentals, lessons, and kids camps are all available.

For snowboarders, a **terrain park** (10 A.M.–9 P.M. daily) has its own chairlift. To access the park, you must purchase a $10 park pass, in addition to your lift ticket.

Mountain Biking

From late May through mid-October, mountain bikers take over the trails at Blue Mountain (705/445-0231 or 877/445-0231, www.bluemountain.ca). The lifts are open to bikers 10 A.M.–8 P.M. daily late June to early September and 10 A.M.–5 P.M. Friday, Saturday, and Sunday in spring and fall. Daily trail passes are $6 (no lift access), $12 (one lift access), or $30 (unlimited lift access). You can rent bikes and safety gear.

If you don't want to hit the trails on your own, a variety of guided mountain-biking options are available, for youth, teens, adults, and families, both novice and experienced riders.

Swimming and Water Sports

If you or your kids love water, check out the **Plunge Aquatic Centre** (200 Mountain Dr., 705/444-8705, www.plungebluemountain.ca, adults $11–13, seniors and children 3–13 $7–10) adjacent to the Westin Trillium House. This year-round water-activity center has indoor and outdoor swimming pools, several water slides, rope swings, hot tubs, and a water playground for toddlers. Schedules vary seasonally, but in general, Plunge is open daily in summer and winter, weekends only in spring and fall. Admission tickets are good for a three-hour period, and prices vary by time of day.

In summer, Blue Mountain Resort maintains a **private beach** (Blue Mountain Activity Central, 705/443-5522 or 800/955-6561) on Georgian Bay, that's open only to resort guests. A complimentary shuttle will take you from the village to the beach; it's about a 10-minute ride.

Accommodations

Blue Mountain Village has several hotel and condominium properties, and just outside the village are additional condo and townhouse complexes. Except for the Westin Trillium House, which you have to contact directly, you can book lodgings through **Blue Mountain Central Reservations** (877/445-0231, www. bluemountain.ca). When booking, ask whether the lodging is ski-in/ski-out or within walking distance of the lifts. Winter room rates typically start at about $150 per night for a double room, and a variety of lodging and lift ticket packages are available.

The **Blue Mountain Inn** was the village's original lodging, and while it's starting to show its age, it offers moderately priced accommodations. You can walk to the Century Express chair lift. For more style, the boutique **Mosaïc** has 163 contemporary suites, ranging from studios to three-bedroom units. The smaller units have kitchenettes, and the larger suites, some of which are multilevel townhouses, have full kitchens. There's a fitness center, as well as a year-round outdoor pool and hot tub. It's not as close to the lifts as the **Weider Lodge** or the **Grand Georgian**—both slightly older condo hotels—but the rooms are more stylish and you can walk to the gondola in a few minutes.

The village's most posh accommodation, located a short walk from the gondola, is the **Westin Trillium House** (220 Mountain Dr., 705/443-8080 or 800/937-8461, www.westinbluemountain.com, $195–550 d), designed like a grand Georgian Bay lodge. The 222 rooms, including standard guest rooms and one-, two-, and three-bedroom suites, have modern furnishings in ski-lodge beiges and browns, as well as TV/DVDs and kitchenettes. There's a 24-hour gym, a year-round outdoor pool, a sauna, and hot tubs, and if you're too tired to walk downstairs to the restaurant or lounge, you can order from room service.

Food

Food in the village tends toward either fuel-up-fast-and-get-back-on-the-slopes fare or simple but hearty pub-style eats. Start your day with coffee and pastry at the **Royal Majesty Espresso Bar Bakery** (190 Jozo Weider Blvd., 705/812-3476, www.royalmajestyatblue.com, generally open 7 A.M.–9 P.M. daily), or stop in later for a bowl of soup or a sandwich. Free Wi-Fi.

A popular après-ski spot, with live music most nights, is **Windy O'Neill's** (170 Jozo Weider Blvd., 705/446-9989, www.windyoneills.com, 11 A.M.–2 A.M. daily, $10–15), an Irish pub that says it's owned by "genuine Irish people." They usually have at least 20 beers on tap, along with basic pub grub, from burgers to fish 'n' chips to traditional Irish stew.

The local outpost of a Toronto-based restaurant group, **Oliver and Bonacini Café Grill** (Westin Trillium House, 220 Mountain Dr., 705/444-8680, www.oliverbonacini.com, 7 A.M.–10 P.M. daily, $13–30) is one of the best places to eat in the village. It's not cheap, but the contemporary dishes are both crowd-pleasing and creative. Try the Japanese-influenced chicken Caesar salad with edamame, shiitake mushrooms, and wasabi peas or the rock shrimp linguine with basil-almond pesto.

Practicalities

The Blue Mountain Resort is 170 kilometers (105 miles) northwest of Toronto and 11 kilometers (7 miles) west of Collingwood, off Highway 26. Depending on traffic and weather conditions, it's about a two-hour drive from metropolitan Toronto. For resort information or reservations, contact **Blue Mountain Resorts Limited** (108 Jozo Weider Blvd., Blue Mountains, ON, 705/445-0231 or 877/445-0231, www.bluemountain.ca) or the **Blue Mountain Village Association** (705/445-0231, www.villageatblue.com).

If you're staying in the Village at Blue Mountain, you don't really need a car. The village is car-free (and ringed with parking lots where you can leave yours). A free **resort shuttle** (www.bluemountain.ca) loops through the village daily every 15–20 minutes between 8 A.M. and 10:30 P.M. Outside of these hours, you can call for a pickup by dialing extension 8280 on any resort phone.

COLLINGWOOD

While many people come to Collingwood to ski or snowboard at nearby Blue Mountain, it's also a pleasant spot for a weekend getaway, even if you're not mountain-bound. The Collingwood area draws gourmets to its many first-rate restaurants. The **Georgian Trail** (705/445-7722, www.brucegreytrails.com) is a flat, 32-kilometer (20-mile) rail trail for hiking and cycling that runs west from Collingwood to the nearby towns of Thornbury and Meaford, passing several beaches en route. In winter, it's a cross-country ski and snowshoeing trail.

To soothe those post-adventure sore muscles, sink into the outdoor baths at the **Scandinave Spa at Blue Mountain** (152 Grey Road 21, Blue Mountains, 705/443-8484 or 877/988-8484, www.scandinave.com, 10 A.M.–9 P.M., $45), which offers a Scandinavian-style "bath experience." First, warm up with heat in one of the Finnish saunas, steam baths, or outdoor hot tubs. Then immerse yourself in a chilling plunge pool. After recovering in one of the relaxation areas, repeat the process until you feel totally tranquil; the average stay is 2–4 hours. The experience is even more magical when snow falls on the hot pools. Bathing suits are required, and you must be at least 19 years old. Prices are $10 less on Wednesdays.

For several days in July, Collingwood is overrun with Elvis Presley lookalikes. The annual **Collingwood Elvis Festival** (866/444-1162, www.collingwoodelvisfestival.com) features a parade, as well as more than 100 tribute concerts. Not only is it the region's biggest event, but it ranks among the world's largest Elvis festivals. If you didn't pack your blue suede shoes, the **Collingwood Music Festival** (519/599-5461, www.collingwoodmusicfestival.com) presents a series of classical and world music concerts in July and August. Performances are held at the New Life Brethren in Christ Church (28 Tracey Lane, at Hurontario St.).

Scenic Caves Nature Adventures

Located high in the hills outside Collingwood, Scenic Caves Nature Adventures (260/280 Scenic Caves Rd., 705/446-0256, www.sceniccaves.com, 9 A.M.–5 P.M. Mon.–Fri., 9 A.M.–6 P.M. Sat.–Sun. May–Oct.) is a sprawling outdoor playground. Walking trails wend through the woods, and you can explore a network of underground caves (try to squeeze yourself through "Fat Man's Misery," a narrow rock channel). A highlight, at least if you're not afraid of heights, is a stroll across the 126-meter (413-foot) suspension bridge, Ontario's longest suspension footbridge, with panoramic views across Georgian Bay. Basic admission rates (adults $20.80, seniors $18.36, and children 3–17 $16.82) include access to the caves, suspension bridge, and walking trails.

If you're more adventurous, consider the three-hour guided eco-tour (adults $95, seniors and children 10–17 $85.), which includes a short hike to the suspension bridge, followed by a treetop canopy tour through the trees on a network of narrow wooden bridges. You'll also tour the caves and whiz through the air on not one, but two, zip lines, including a 305-meter (1,000-foot) plunge from the top of the Niagara Escarpment.

In winter, the eco-tours aren't offered, but the park is open for cross-country skiing and snowshoeing (9 A.M.–5 P.M. daily Dec.–Mar., full-day weekend/weekday pass: adults $18.50/14.50, seniors and children 6–17 $14.50/$12.50). You can even snowshoe across the suspension bridge. Ski and snowshoe rentals are available, and on weekends, you can purchase a half-day admission (adults $16.50, seniors/children $12.50).

Allow a minimum of two hours to explore the site, but you can easily spend most of the day. Wear running or hiking shoes. There's a small snack bar, but for more variety, pack your own picnic lunch.

Accommodations

A number of Collingwood's restored Victorian homes are now inns or B&Bs, and in the hills around town, you'll find more small accommodations. Contact the **Collingwood Area Bed and Breakfast Association** (www.bbcanada.com/associations/cabba) for additional lodging options. Motels are clustered along Highway 26, west of town. Most area lodgings are open year-round.

The **Beild House Country Inn** (64 Third St., 705/444-1522 or 888/322-3453, www.beildhouse.com, $140 d) isn't in the country—it's just a block from Collingwood's main downtown street—but it has the faded charm of a country estate. The parlor, with its dark woodwork, chintz sofas, and portraits of Victorian gentlemen, and the dining room, where elaborate multicourse dinners are served by candlelight, recall its glory days as a private residence (it was built in 1909). Drawing couples who come to cocoon, the 11 guest rooms are romantic in a cozy, if slightly fussy, Victorian style. Rates start at $140 for a double room including a full breakfast and afternoon tea; on weekends, guests must also include dinner ($60 per person). If you're not staying at the inn, you can have dinner here with advance reservations.

As the name might suggest, the four guest rooms at the romantic **Bacchus House** (142 Hume St., 705/446-4700, www.bacchushouse.ca, call for rates) are decorated with a wine theme. All the bedrooms in this 1880 yellow-brick Victorian have hardwood floors, TV/DVD players, and iPod docking stations, but each has slightly different features: the purple Pinot Noir Suite has an ornate four-poster bed, the Merlot Suite (done in brown and burgundy) has a gas fireplace, and the Cabernet Sauvignon Suite has a clawfoot tub. There are several common spaces for guests, including the living room with a fireplace and overstuffed sofas, a den with a TV, a deck with a hot tub, and the dining room, where a full

breakfast is served. Only the location on a busy street mars the elegance of this upscale lodging; if you're sensitive to traffic noise, choose the golden-hued Chardonnay Suite at the rear of the house.

Set on a 15-acre property with gardens, walking trails, a swimming pool, and a gaggle of ducks and hens, the **Willow Trace B&B** (7833 Poplar Side Rd., 705/445-9003, www.collingwoodbedandbreakfast.com, $125–150 d) feels like a rural getaway, yet it's only a five-minute drive from downtown. The rooms are bright and modern, with two upstairs and one on the lower level facing the gardens (the downstairs room is family-friendly). Co-owner and chef Philip Tarlo runs the B&B with his wife Leanne Calvert and allows guests to choose from a menu of breakfast options that he'll prepare to order—perhaps cinnamon French toast, a customized omelet, or a full English breakfast.

Food

Collingwood's restaurants range from the foodie to the ardently epicurean. Most are located on or near Hurontario Street in the town center. Even hot dogs go gourmet at **Buddha Dog** (48 Pine St., 705/444-2005, www.buddhafoodha.com), which upgrades the lowly tube steak with locally raised beef and homemade buns.

Hidden in a lane downtown, **Tesoro** (18 School House Ln., 705/444-9230, lunch and dinner Mon.–Sat., dinner only Sun., $14–27), with its sturdy pine tables and vibrant red chairs, is the sort of welcoming, casual Italian eatery everyone would like to have in their neighborhood. There's a long list of creative pizzas (try the Tre Funghi with black olives and three types of mushrooms), as well as updated versions of Italian classics, like penne *arrabiatta* (pasta with spicy sausage and hot peppers), chicken *parmigiano,* or lasagna.

One of Ontario's most distinctive dining destinations is ◖ **Eigensinn Farm** (449357 Concession Rd. 10, Singhampton, 519/922-3128), which draws well-heeled gourmets from far and wide. Chef-owner Michael Stadtlander left Toronto for a quieter country life here; he accommodates no more than a dozen diners per night, creating extravagant eight-course tasting menus ($275). And that's not including wine (the restaurant has no liquor license, so guests must bring their own). The restaurant's schedule can be as wildly personal as the dining experience, so make reservations well in advance. To get here from Collingwood, take County Road 124 south for about 13 kilometers (eight miles).

The owners of Eigensinn Farm also run the nearby **Haisai Restaurant & Bakery** (794079 County Rd. 124, Singhampton, 705/445-2748, www.haisairestaurantbakery.com). The bakery (8:30 A.M.–6 P.M. Wed.–Sat., 9 A.M.–6 P.M. Sun.) sells freshly baked breads, buns, and pastries, along with a selection of prepared foods. The restaurant (Fri.–Sat. evenings) serves elaborate multicourse tasting menus by reservation only. No credit cards.

Practicalities

The **Georgian Triangle Tourist Association** (30 Mountain Rd., 705/445-7722 or 888/227-8667, www.visitsouthgeorgianbay.ca) runs a tourist information center that provides information about the Collingwood/Blue Mountain region. **Greyhound Bus Lines** (800/661-8747, www.greyhound.ca) operates two buses a day in each direction between Toronto and Collingwood; the same buses also go on to Blue Mountain. The trip takes about 3 hours. In town, the buses depart from Collingwood's **Transportation Centre** (22 Second St., 705/445-7095). On the mountain, buses stop at the **Blue Mountain Inn** (www.bluemountain.ca).

Simcoe County Airport Service (137 Brock St., Barrie, 705/728-1148 or 800/461-7529, www.simcoecountyairportservice.ca) runs regular vans from Toronto's Pearson airport to Collingwood and the Blue Mountain Resort. Prices vary depending on the number of people in your party. From Pearson to Collingwood, the one-way price is $88 for one person, $119 for two; to Blue Mountain, it's $99 for one, $130 for two. **Colltrans** (705/446-

1196, www.collingwood.ca, 7 A.M.–6 P.M. Mon.–Sat., 9 A.M.–5 P.M. Sun., $1) is the town's public-transportation service, with three routes around the community (but not out to Blue Mountain). The main bus "terminal" (Second St. at Pine St.) is an outdoor bus shelter.

VICINITY OF COLLINGWOOD

Several small towns around Collingwood, including Thornbury and Meaford to the west and Creemore to the south, are worth exploring for their galleries, shops, and restaurants. Wasaga Beach, the world's longest freshwater beach, is also an easy day trip from Collingwood.

Creemore

This village of about 1,300 people makes a great day trip if you're looking for that elusive "small-town charm." The main downtown street—Mill Street—is lined with art galleries, cafés, and shops, ready-made for wandering and browsing. Creemore's main "tourist attraction" is the **Creemore Springs Brewery** (139 Mill St., 705/466-2240 or 800/267-2240, www.creemoresprings.com, 10 A.M.–6 P.M. Mon.–Sat., 11 A.M.–5 P.M. Sun.), which was started in 1987 by three beer-loving guys who retired to the area and decided they needed a hobby. The brewery now produces several varieties of beer, including their signature Creemore Springs Premium Lager. You can take a free 30-minute tour of their production facility, which wraps up with a beer tasting. Tours are offered several times a day year-round. The brewery shop sells beer and brew-related souvenirs.

The **Mad and Noisy Gallery** (154 Mill St., 705/466-5555, www.madandnoisy.com, 11 A.M.–5 P.M. Mon.–Fri., 10 A.M.–5 P.M. Sat., noon–4 P.M. Sun.) is neither—it's named for the two rivers that meet near Creemore. It showcases high-quality work of painters, sculptors, photographers, and other artists, most of whom hail from the Southern Georgian Bay area. The **Maplestone Gallery** (142 Mill St., 705/520-0067, http://maplestonegallery.com, 11 A.M.–5 P.M. Thurs.–Fri., 10 A.M.–5 P.M. Sat., 11 A.M.–4 P.M. Sun.) is unique in Canada

The Creemore Jail is North America's smallest prison.

for displaying only contemporary mosaic art. Many of the works are surprisingly ornate and, not surprisingly, beautiful. Want to learn to create mosaics yourself? The gallery runs periodic workshops for beginners.

Mill Street has several café's, bakeries, and restaurants, as well as the **100 Mile Store** (176 Mill St., 705/466-3514, www.100milestore. ca), a local grocery that lives up to its name by sourcing its products—from produce to grains to meats—within 100 miles of town. Stop in for locally made snacks, cheeses, or ice cream. A good choice for a sit-down meal is **Chez Michel** (150 Mill St., 705/466-3331, www.chezmichel.ca, lunch and dinner Wed.– Sun., $26–60), decorated in sunny yellows and bright Provençal blues. The kitchen uses local Ontario ingredients to create classic French dishes from *escargots* (snails) to *steak au poivre*.

When you're done shopping and snacking, venture east of Mill Street to find the **Creemore Jail** (Library St., between Elizabeth and Caroline Sts.). This diminutive stone structure, built in 1892, claims to be the smallest jail in North America.

Creemore is about 30 kilometers (19 miles) southeast of Collingwood. If you're not in a hurry, you can meander here through the countryside along a series of back roads. Otherwise, the fastest route is to take Highway 26 east from Collingwood to Highway 42 south; then go west on Highway 9 into Creemore and turn left onto Mill Street.

Wasaga Beach

The Wasaga area played a role in the War of 1812, through a trading ship called the *Nancy*, built in 1789. In 1814, American troops attacked the Nancy on the Nottawasaga River. The ship sank, and eventually the silt and sand flowing through the river collected around the ship's hull, forming an island. Today, at the **Nancy Island Historic Site** (late May–early Sept., 705/429-2728, www.wasagabeachpark. com), you can see the *Nancy*'s hull, watch a video about her story, and join in as park staff reenact elements of the *Nancy*'s history.

Along Georgian Bay east of Collingwood, **Wasaga Beach Provincial Park** (11 22nd St. N., Wasaga Beach, 705/429-2516, www.ontarioparks.com, 8:15 A.M.–10 P.M. daily Apr.–mid-Oct., $13–18/vehicle) is the world's longest freshwater beach. This stretch of sand extends for 14 kilometers (nearly nine miles) and is divided into eight different sections, each with a different personality. Beaches 1–4 are closer into town and have more restaurants, shops, and other services; they're also more crowded and honky-tonk. As you move farther from the town center—to Beaches 5 and 6 to the south and New Wasaga and Allenwood Beaches to the north—the sand becomes less populated and more peaceful. Because the beach is flat and the bay is shallow, Wasaga is a popular destination for families. (Note that a new Wasaga Beach Welcome Centre is slated to open in 2012).

Although most people come for the beach, Wasaga also has 50 kilometers (31 miles) of hiking trails. The park service leads guided hikes on Wednesdays in July and August. In winter, there are 30 kilometers (19 miles) of trails for cross-country skiing. Access the trail network from the **Wasaga Nordic Centre** (705/429-0943, 9 A.M.–5 P.M. daily mid-Dec.–mid-Mar., adults $9.50, children 6–17 $4.75).

For information about Wasaga Beach, contact the provincial park office (705/429-2516, www.ontarioparks.com), or check the informative **Friends of Wasaga Beach** (www.wasagabeachpark.com) website. The **Town of Wasaga Beach** (705/429-3844, www.wasagabeach.com) and the **Wasaga Beach Chamber of Commerce** (705/429-2247 or 866/292-7242, www.wasagainfo.com) are good sources of information about accommodations and services in the Wasaga area. Wasaga Beach has the usual assortment of modest beach motels, as well as privately run campgrounds (the provincial park has no camping facilities). Cottage rentals are also popular; contact the Chamber of Commerce (705/429-2247 or 866/292-7242, www.wasagainfo.com) for details.

Located about 20 kilometers (12.5 miles) east of Collingwood, Wasaga Beach is an easy day trip from the Collingwood area; take Highway 26 to Highway 92.

Midland and Parry Sound

This peninsula on Georgian Bay's southwestern side houses the towns of Midland and Penetanguishene. It once played an important role in Ontario's early history. Long populated by First Nations people, in the 1600s a site near present-day Midland became the region's first European settlement, when a group of French Jesuits established a village there. The area retains a strong French and First Nations heritage. Several interesting historic sites, particularly the well-designed Sainte-Marie among the Hurons, illuminate the region's past.

Like the other areas around Georgian Bay, the Midland region has its share of beautiful outdoor destinations, particularly Wye Marsh in Midland and the large Awenda Provincial Park in Penetanguishene. It's also a gateway to the 30,000 Islands that dot Georgian Bay, some of which are protected in the Georgian Bay Islands National Park.

You can visit the Georgian Bay Islands National Park in a day trip from either Midland or Penetanguishene; it's less than an hour's drive to Honey Harbour, where the boat to the park islands departs.

North along Georgian Bay is Parry Sound, a pleasant community that's both a base for outdoor activities and a cultural destination. Less than an hour's drive away, the ruggedly beautiful Killbear Provincial Park draws travelers to its waterfront campgrounds.

MIDLAND
The largest community along this part of Georgian Bay, Midland is still a fairly small town (population 17,000), and it retains its low-

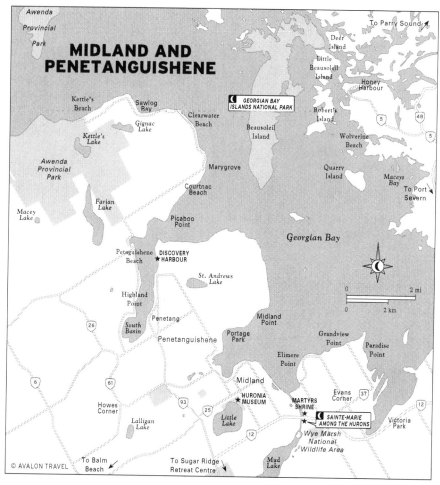

key feel along King Street, the main downtown street. The town has begun to sprawl out from the center, with malls and other developments on its edges, and its sights are spread out around the area. But it's a convenient base for exploring the region's mix of historic and outdoor attractions.

As you walk around downtown Midland, be on the lookout for the 34 **murals** (www.downtownmidland.ca) painted on walls around town. One mural, painted on silos along Midland Harbor, depicts a Jesuit priest and a Huron native at Sainte-Marie; it is reportedly the largest outdoor historic mural in North America. Pick up a mural map at the **Southern Georgian Bay Chamber of Commerce** (208 King St., 705/526-7884) or contact the **Downtown Midland Business Improvement Association** (212 King St., 705/527-7246, www.downtownmidland.ca), which offers free guided mural tours by appointment.

◖ Sainte-Marie Among the Hurons

In 1639, a group of French Jesuit missionaries

began constructing a community near present-day Midland, establishing the first European settlement in Ontario. Their goal was to bring Christianity to the native Wendat people, whom they called the "Huron." The Jesuits worked with the Huron for 10 years, until hostilities worsened between the Huron and the nearby Iroquois people. After the Iroquois killed two of the priests, the Jesuits abandoned the settlement and burned it to the ground to protect it from desecration. Centuries later, in 1930, Pope Pius XI canonized the murdered priests, Father Jean de Brébeuf and Father Gabriel Lalemant.

What you see today at this fascinating historic village (Hwy. 12 E., 705/526-7838, www.saintemarieamongthehurons.on.ca, 10 A.M.–5 P.M. daily mid-May–mid-Oct., 10 A.M.–5 P.M. Mon.–Fri. late Apr.–mid-May and late Oct., adults $11.25, seniors $9.25, students $9.75, children 6–12 $8.50) is a "re-imagination" of the 17th-century settlement. Because the Jesuits left no records, historians can only theorize what the community actually looked like. It wasn't until the 1940s and '50s that archeologists began excavating the area, providing clues to the village's history and structure.

Sainte-Marie was reconstructed replicating French construction styles of the period. Surrounded by a high wooden fence, the settlement has 25 buildings in three main areas. The **North Court** was the mission's primary living and working quarters, including a cookhouse, chapel, carpentry shop, a chicken run, and stables. The **South Court** was where supplies arrived (following an 800-mile canoe journey from Quebec). The South Court includes a reconstructed waterway with working locks that may have allowed canoes to enter the mission from the river. The third section of the settlement was the **Native Area,** where a church, a longhouse, a hospital, and other structures illustrate the mix of French and Huron building styles and cultures.

You can easily spend several hours exploring the settlement. Start your visit with the 15-minute movie that introduces the site's history. In summer, costumed guides staff the village buildings, demonstrating elements of village life, from cooking to blacksmithing to Wendat storytelling. In spring or fall, when fewer staff are on duty, rent the audio guide ($3) to help understand the site. Following your walk through the village, you can explore museum exhibits that provide more background and history about the settlement.

Sainte-Marie Among the Hurons (www.saintemarieamongthehurons.on.ca) organizes a number of special events throughout the year. Highlights include the annual **Aboriginal Festival** (June), which honors the Hurons' heritage with traditional dancing, music, games, and crafts, and the **First Light Festival** (late Nov.), which lights up the Sainte-Marie site with more than 3,000 candles.

The site is five kilometers (three miles) east on Highway 12 from the intersection of Highway 93.

Wye Marsh Wildlife Centre

A lovely spot to enjoy the outdoors is this nature center and marshlands (16160 Hwy. 12 E., 705/526-7809, www.wyemarsh.com, 9 A.M.–5 P.M. daily, adults $11, seniors and students $8.50, children 6–12 $8) on the east side of Midland, next to Sainte-Marie Among the Hurons. The visitor center has exhibits about local ecology, and kids enjoy the live animal presentations, but the real action is outdoors, where one can follow a network of walking trails around the marsh. Rent an audio guide for details about the plants and wildlife, or simply follow the interpretive signs and climb up the observation tower for views over the marsh.

The marsh is a nesting habitat for trumpeter swans, and one highlight of a visit here is the chance to observe these majestic birds. You can canoe or kayak on the channels that wend through the marsh, and guided canoe excursions are offered.

In winter, there are 22 kilometers (14 miles) of groomed trails for cross-country skiing and 10 kilometers (six miles) of snowshoeing trails. Ski ($15) and snowshoe rentals ($5–10) are available. You can also take a snowshoe eco-tour, a three-hour guided walk to learn about the local waterfowl, plants, and wetlands. A wide variety of other nature programs are offered throughout the year.

Martyrs' Shrine

Located across the highway from Sainte-Marie Among the Hurons, this 1926 church (16163 Hwy. 12 W., 705/526-3788, www.martyrs-shrine.com, 8:30 A.M.–9 P.M. daily mid-May–mid-Oct., adults and children 10 and older $4), with its two soaring spires, honors the memory of the Jesuits who worked at Sainte-Marie but were killed in a 1649 Iroquois raid. Mass is celebrated several times a day, and you can stroll around the gardens and walkways. The site draws religious pilgrims from all over the world. An onsite café serves basic breakfasts and lunches.

Huronia Museum

Exploring the Huronia Museum (549 Little Lake Park, 705/526-2844, www.huroniamuseum.com, 9 A.M.–5 P.M. daily May–Oct., Mon.–Fri. Nov.–Apr., adults $8.60, seniors $7.55, children 5–17 $5.40), an old-fashioned regional history museum, feels like a treasure hunt. You might find everything from washtubs to wheelchairs, sewing machines to the "Slenderizer" (an old-time exercise machine). Most of the hodgepodge of artifacts dates from the 1800s and 1900s. Also on the site is the Huron Ouendat Village, a modest re-creation of a 16th-century First Nations settlement.

Sports and Recreation

The Midland/Penetanguishene peninsula is surrounded by water, but many of the beaches are private. One exception is the small, sandy **Balm Beach** (www.visitbalmbeach.com) on Georgian Bay. From Midland, take Highway 25/Balm Beach Road directly west to the water. The west-facing beach is a pretty spot to watch the sunset. The **Miss Midland 30,000 Islands Boat Cruises** (705/549-3388, www.midlandtours.com, mid-May–mid-Oct., adults $27, seniors $25, students $20, children 5–14 $14) are two-hour tours around the Georgian Bay Islands

National Park and some of the other 30,000 islands. Cruises depart from the Midland Town Dock at the foot of King Street.

Accommodations

Midland has the usual selection of chain motels, clustered along King Street near Highway 12 or on Yonge Street off Highway 93. Try the **Best Western Highland Inn** (924 King St., 705/526-9307 or 800/461-4265, www.bestwesternmidland.com) or the **Midland Comfort Inn** (980 King St., 705/526-2090 or 888/274-3020, www.comfortinnmidland.com). For bed-and-breakfast options, check the website for the **Southern Georgian Bay B&B Association** (www.southerngeorgianbaybb.com).

Want to get away from it all? Set amid tall grasses and marshlands on a secluded country road and about a 15-minute drive south of downtown Midland, the ☾ **Sugar Ridge Retreat Centre** (5720 Forgets Rd., Wyebridge, 705/528-1793 or 866/609-1793, www.sugar-ridge.ca, $120/night with breakfast) may be one of the quietest places you'll ever stay. While many guests come for yoga retreats and other workshops, artists, writers, and anyone looking for a peaceful escape is also welcome. Ten sturdy cabins dot the fields around the main lodge building, a contemporary Zen-style retreat center with an airy yoga studio, guest lounge, and large dining room. The cabins, which sleep up to four, are simply furnished with warm duvets, electric heat, and ceiling fans. They have no plumbing, phones, or Internet service; however, the area does have cell phone coverage, and restrooms, showers, and Wi-Fi are available in the lodge, where vegetarian meals are also served. Rates vary depending on the number of guests and meals, and whether you're part of a group retreat. Guests are welcome to join in yoga and meditation classes (drop-in fee $15). Owners Liz and Kurt Frost, both psychotherapists and yoga instructors, also accommodate B&B guests in their home down the road (5790 Forgets Rd., $95–115 d).

Food

For places to eat in Midland, wander along

King Street downtown. At **Ciboulette et Cie** (248 King St., 705/245-0410, www.ciboulet-teetcie.ca, 8:30–9 A.M. until 6–7 P.M. daily; call for specific hours), a cheerful café and takeout shop (the name is French for "Chive and Company"), the day starts with freshly baked scones and other pastries. Then creative sandwiches and delicious ready-to-eat salads, perhaps Brussels sprout slaw or roasted sweet potatoes with cranberries, make a quick lunch or early supper.

With its walls of books, maps, and photos of faraway lands, **The Explorers Cafe** (345 King St., 705/527-9199, www.theexplorerscafe.com, noon–10 P.M. Tues.–Sat., lunch $10–12, dinner $17–25) resembles a Victorian-era adventurer's residence. The menu wanders the world, too; there's always an Indian-style curry and a New Zealand meat pie, and you might find an Argentinean steak, Spanish grilled sardines, or a Singapore noodle bowl. Despite the international emphasis, there's usually a "100 mile meal," as well, with most of its ingredients sourced locally. Although the restaurant is right downtown, you may need a compass to find it, since it's set back from the main road; look for their signboard on King Street.

Craving Texas-style barbecued pork ribs? Jerk chicken? BBQ brisket? Then head for the little yellow bungalow, about 10 minutes south of Midland, that houses **MAD Michael's Restaurant and Bakery** (8215 Hwy. 93, Wyebridge, 705/527-1666, www.madmichaels.com, noon–8 P.M. Thurs.–Sun. May–mid-Oct., lunch $13–16, dinner $15–20). This isn't any ordinary BBQ shack; chef "Mad Michael" White smokes ribs in his outdoor kitchen, bakes bread, and even makes his own ketchup (in his spare time, he crafts rustic wood furniture). Save room for a slice of homemade pie.

Practicalities

The helpful staff at the **Southern Georgian Bay Chamber of Commerce and Tourism Information Centre** (208 King St., 705/526-7884 or 800/263-7745, www.southerngeorgianbay.on.ca) in downtown Midland can provide lots of information about the region.

The Midland/Penetanguishene area is about 160 kilometers (100 miles) from Toronto. From Highway 93, take Highway 12 east, then turn left onto King Street for downtown Midland or continue east on Highway 12 to Sainte-Marie Among the Hurons, the Martyrs' Shrine, and Wye Marsh. The attractions in Midland and Penetanguishene are spread out over a fairly wide area. It's difficult to explore the region without a car.

PENETANGUISHENE

Smaller than nearby Midland, the town of Penetanguishene (population 9,300) has a strong French heritage; roughly 16 percent of the residents speak French as their first language. Penetanguishene's main attractions are the restored naval base at Discovery Harbour and the sprawling Awenda Provincial Park, which has the region's best beaches. Penetanguishene Harbor is also the departure point for the area's most interesting 30,000 Islands cruise.

Discovery Harbour

Following the War of 1812, the British built a naval base at Penetanguishene to protect the Upper Great Lakes region from possible future American attacks. Today, you can visit the restored base now known as Discovery Harbour (93 Jury Dr., 705/549-8064, www.discoveryharbour.on.ca, 10 A.M.–5 P.M. daily July–early Sept.; 10 A.M.–5 P.M. Mon.–Fri. late May–June, adults $6, seniors and students $5.25, children 6–12 $4.25) to learn more about naval and military life here in the 1800s. While only one original building remains (the 1845 Officers' Quarters), the reconstructed site reflects life on the base during the period from 1817 to 1822. Guides in period costumes conduct tours of the 19 historic buildings and demonstrate various aspects of sailors' life, from cooking to ropework to games. You can also tour replicas of two majestic 18th-century British sailing vessels, the H.M.S. *Bee,* a supply schooner, and the H.M.S. *Tecumseth,* a warship.

Awenda Provincial Park

Fronting Georgian Bay 11 kilometers (seven

miles) northwest of Penetanguishene, this 2,915-hectare (7,200-acre) provincial park (Awenda Park Rd., off Concession Rd. 16 E./ Lafontaine Rd. E., 705/549-2231, www.ontarioparks.com, $13/vehicle) is a beautiful destination for hiking and swimming. One of the largest parks in central Ontario, Awenda is in a transition zone between north and south, making it home to a diverse array of plants and trees, as well as roughly 200 bird species and many reptiles and amphibians. In summer, park staff offer a variety of nature programs, theatrical productions, and other special events; call the park office or check online (Friends of Awenda, www.awendapark.ca) for schedules.

Awenda is open year-round, and you can cross-country ski here in winter.

30,000 Island Cruises

What makes the island cruises special on the **M.S. *Georgian Queen*** (705/549-7795 or 800/363-7447, www.georgianbaycruises.com, May–mid-Oct., adults $20–27, seniors $18–24, children 5–14 $9–11) is the onboard commentary that the companionable captain provides. As you cruise out of Penetanguishene Harbor and out among the 30,000 Islands, Captain Steve will not only point out the "sights," but he'll tell you who lives on what island (many are private), which properties are for sale (and at what price), and how locals manage to build homes, transport goods, and spend summers on these isolated chunks of rock. The cruises depart from the Town Docks at the foot of Main Street and range from 1–3 hours. Take one of the longer cruises if you can, since the shortest excursions stay in the harbor area rather than travel out to the islands.

Sports and Recreation

Awenda Provincial Park (Awenda Park Rd., off Concession Rd. 16 E./Lafontaine Rd. E., 705/549-2231, www.ontarioparks.com, $13/vehicle) has approximately 30 kilometers (19 miles) of multiuse trails throughout the park. The most popular is the easy **Beach Trail,** which connects the park's four beaches. Off the Beach Trail, you can follow the easy, one-

kilometer (0.6-mile) **Beaver Pond Trail,** most of which is along a boardwalk, to an area that had extensive beaver activity.

Longer park trails include: the **Robitaille Homestead Trail,** a three-kilometer (1.9-mile) round-trip trail past ancient sand dunes, that begins in the day parking lot near Bear Campground; the five-kilometer (three-mile) **Wendat Trail,** which starts near Kettle's Lake; and the 13-kilometer (eight-mile) **Bluff Trail,** which circles the campgrounds and connects the camping areas to the beach.

Some of the nicest swimming spots in the Midland/Penetanguishene area are within the provincial park, which has four beaches along Georgian Bay. **First Beach,** closest to the parking area, is a sheltered, family-friendly sand beach that also has rocks for the kids to climb on. You can continue along the beach trail to **Second Beach; Third Beach,** which has particularly soft sand; and eventually to the more secluded **Fourth Beach.** It's about two kilometers (1.25 miles) from First to Fourth Beach.

You can also swim at **Kettle's Lake,** an inland lake with an easy boardwalk trail to the water. The lake is also a calm spot for canoeing, particularly for beginning paddlers; in summer, canoe rentals are available. Around the lake, you might see otters, beaver, loon, or great blue heron.

Entertainment and Events

Located at Discovery Harbour, the **King's Wharf Theatre** (97 Jury Dr., 705/549-5555 or 888/449-4463, www.draytonentertainment.com) is a professional summer theater that produces several plays every year between June and early September. Discovery Harbour celebrates the region's Métis traditions through music, art, and games at the annual **Métis Day Bo'jou Neejee event** (early Aug., www.discoveryharbour.on.ca). The Métis are an aboriginal group of mixed First Nations and European heritage; more than 10 percent of Penetanguishene's current population is of Métis descent.

Accommodations and Food

Catering primarily to boaters and their guests,

the **Hindson Marina Floatel-Motel** (79 Champlain Rd., 705/549-2991, www.hindsonmarine.on.ca, $109–132 d) is a floating lodging, right on the docks on the west side of Penetanguishene Harbor. The three rooms and one two-room suite are ordinary motel units, but you can't get much closer to the water than this. Entrance is through the marina gates.

Surrounded by lush gardens and tall pines, the **Copeland Woods B&B** (47 Copeland Creek Dr., 705/549-1330, www.copelandwoodsbb.com, May–Oct., $115–135 d) feels like an escape into nature. Because the owners built the home as a combination residence and B&B, the accommodations are well designed for guests. Of the three stylish-country guest rooms, one is on the main level, and the other two are on the lower level facing the garden and woods. There's a kitchenette with a fridge and microwave for guests' use, and a full breakfast is served either on the deck or around the Arts and Crafts–style dining table. The B&B is in a quiet residential subdivision on Penetanguishene's west side.

Do you fantasize about having your own cottage right on Georgian Bay? Awenda Provincial Park's **Stone Cottage** (Awenda Park Rd., off Concession Rd. 16 E./Lafontaine Rd. E., 705/549-2231, www.ontarioparks.com, May–Oct.) can be yours, at least for a week or two. Down an unmarked lane deep in the park, the lodging looks like the classic Canadian hideaway, made of solid fieldstone, with a spacious terrace directly above the water. Inside, the huge open living room has a stone fireplace and a wall of windows facing the bay. There are two bedrooms, one with a double bed and two bunks and a second with twin beds. So what's not to love? Like the classic cottages of the 1940s, when the Stone Cottage was built, it has no running water; large jugs of drinking water are provided, and there's an outhouse but no shower. You also need to bring sleeping bags or linens, as well as food and cooking gear. The cottage rents by the week ($1,040/week) from late June through early September; you can book stays of two days or more ($150/night) in the spring or fall. Make reservations (Ontario Parks Reservation Service, 888/668-7275, www.ontarioparks.com, $8.50

for online bookings, $9.50 for telephone bookings) well in advance.

Just up the hill from Penetanguishene harbor, the **Froth Café** (102 Main St., 705/549-7199, www.frothcafe.com, 8 A.M.–5 P.M. Tues.–Sun.) is a convenient spot for breakfast, lunch, or a sightseeing coffee break. The menu is simple: scones, bagels, French toast, and omelets in the morning (all under $5); salads and sandwiches ($6–10), including a warm chicken panini, at midday. Jazz on the stereo and local art on the walls make it feel cool and arty. Free Wi-Fi.

CAMPING

The six campgrounds at **Awenda Provincial Park** (Awenda Park Rd., off Concession Rd. 16 E./Lafontaine Rd. E., 705/549-2231, www.ontarioparks.com, mid-May–mid-Oct., $36.75 tent sites, $42.25 electrical sites) are set amid maple and oak forests, so the 333 shaded sites feel comparatively private. All the camping areas have flush toilets and showers, and three have laundry facilities. Although the park has lovely beaches, none of the campgrounds is on the water. The Snake, Wolf, and Deer areas are closest to the bay, but it's still a long walk. Bring bicycles if you can. To book a campsite, contact the Ontario Parks Reservation Service (888/668-7275, www.ontarioparks.com, $8.50 for online bookings, $9.50 for telephone bookings).

Practicalities

The **Penetanguishene Tourist Information Centre** (1 Main St., 705/549-2232, www.penetanguishene.ca, 10 A.M.–6 P.M. Wed.–Sun. mid-to-late May, 10 A.M.–6 P.M. daily June and Sept., 10 A.M.–8 P.M. daily July–Aug.) is at the town docks.

The Midland/Penetanguishene area is about 160 kilometers (100 miles) from Toronto. Highway 93 connects Midland to Penetanguishene, where it becomes Main Street. You really need a car to explore the region.

◖ THE GEORGIAN BAY ISLANDS NATIONAL PARK

Georgian Bay is dotted with at least 30,000 islands. Some are not much more than a big

THAT'S A LOT OF ISLANDS

Many people outside of Ontario know about the Thousand Islands, the chain of islands along the St. Lawrence River in the eastern part of the province. After all, there's even a salad dressing with the Thousand Islands name. Yet the Georgian Bay region has far more than just a thousand isles. Depending on who's counting, Georgian Bay is dotted with at least 30,000 islands. It's one of the world's largest freshwater archipelagoes.

Some of these islands are hardly more than specks of bare rock, while others are quite substantial. Manitoulin Island, which measures 2,765 square kilometers (1,067 square miles) on the bay's northern side, is the largest freshwater island in the world.

What created these many different islands? During the ice age, more than 10,000 years ago, glaciers covered what is now Canada. According to one theory, the movement of these glaciers compressed and reshaped the land, fashioning the distinctive landscape of islands and coves that today surrounds Georgian Bay.

UNESCO has recognized the unique geography of the Georgian Bay region and its islands, designating 347,000 hectares (857,455 acres) of the shoreline between the Severn and French Rivers as the **Georgian Bay Biosphere Reserve** (705/774-0978 or 866/495-4227, www.gbbr.ca). One of 15 such reserves in Canada, it's home to more than 100 species of at-risk animals and plants, including the eastern wolf, the lake sturgeon, and the Massasauga rattlesnake. The biosphere's mission is to assist in the conservation of these species and to support both education and sustainable development in the region, working with the provincial and national parks, local municipalities, and private businesses and landowners along the bay.

The 30,000 Islands are a mix of public and private lands. Some, like the 63 islands of the **Georgian Bay Islands National Park** (705/526-9804, www.pc.gc.ca) or **Fathom Five National Marine Park** (519/596-2233, www.pc.gc.ca), are government-protected natural areas. Many others are privately owned, with a cottage or two offering their owners a waterfront getaway. Visitors to this island region can cruise around the bays and harbors, explore the island parks, and even soar above the islands by floatplane.

So come back again and again. To tour even a tiny fraction of these 30,000 islands will take you years – no, decades – of exploring.

---

rock jutting out of the water, while others are substantial enough to house entire communities. A visit to Georgian Bay Islands National Park (www.pc.gc.ca, open year-round), established in 1929 and encompassing 63 islands across Georgian Bay, is perhaps the easiest way to sample the island experience.

With numerous hiking trails, beaches, and campgrounds, as well as a visitor center, Beausoleil Island, the largest of the park's islands, is the most accessible area. Parks Canada runs a seasonal boat service from Honey Harbour to Beausoleil to take day-trippers to the island (in fact, the boat is named *DayTripper*). To reach islands other than Beausoleil Island, you need to have your own boat, make arrangements with a local outfitter, or hire a water taxi.

Most of the boats traversing the islands are powerboats. While experienced kayakers and canoeists can explore the park islands on their own, the park service advises extreme caution, due to the frequently heavy boat traffic and to the many rocks just under the surface that can surprise the unwary. The park service has partnered with **White Squall Paddling Centre** (19 James St., Parry Sound, 705/746-4936, www.whitesquall.com) to offer guided kayak day trips to some of the park's northern islands.

Honey Harbour is the jumping-off point to visit the park. It's about 168 kilometers (104 miles) northwest of Toronto and 35 kilometers (22 miles) northwest of Midland, the nearest major town.

Georgian Bay Islands National Park is technically open year-round, but park services, including boat transportation between Honey Harbour and Beausoleil Island, operate only between mid-May and mid-October.

Beausoleil Island

The main destination for visitors exploring the Georgian Bay Islands National Park (www. pc.gc.ca, open year-round) is this 11-square-kilometer (4.2 square mile) island, 15 minutes by boat from the Parks Canada marina in Honey Harbour. A unique feature of Beausoleil Island is that it encompasses two different natural environments. The northern part of the island is typical of the Canadian Shield, which extends into Northern Ontario, with its rocky shoreline and its windblown juniper and pine forests. On Beausoleil's southern half, you'll see more hardwood trees, especially maples, beech, oak, and birch, and land that's grassy or marshy, rather than rocky. The best sandy beaches are on the southern end, but you can swim almost anywhere that looks inviting.

Bring your own food and water, along with anything else you need for the day (hiking shoes, swim suit, towel, and insect repellent). While park rangers are on duty on Beausoleil Island during the summer months, there are no snack bars or other services.

Beausoleil Island has about a dozen marked hiking trails, ranging from a 0.3-kilometer (0.2-mile) passage across the island's narrowest point, to an 8.2-kilometer (5-mile) path that traverses between the island's north and south. Most are for hikers only, but bicycles are allowed on two of the routes. Pick up a copy of the park *Visitor Guide,* available free at any of the park offices or at the Beausoleil information kiosk. It includes a trail map with trail distances and approximate hiking times.

Parks Canada runs the **DayTripper** boat service (705/526-8907, adults $15.70, seniors $13.45, children 6–16 $11.70) to transport visitors from Honey Harbour to Beausoleil Island. The *DayTripper* makes the 15-minute trip several times a day (except Wednesdays) in July and August and on Saturdays in the spring and fall. The *DayTripper* rates include park admission. Reservations are recommended.

Two privately owned water taxis also shuttle visitors from Honey Harbour to the park's islands: **Georgian Bay Water Services** (705/627-3062, www.gbws.ca) and **Honey Harbour Boat Club** (705/756-2411). If you take a water taxi to Beausoleil, park admission is $5.80 for adults, $4.90 for seniors, and $2.90 for children 6–16.

Accommodations and Food

Within the national park, the only accommodation option is camping. If you don't want to camp, you'll need to stay on the mainland. The village of Honey Harbour, where the park service boat dock is located, has a handful of places to stay and eat. Most are seasonal, opening in late May or June and closing in September or October. Port Severn is a blink-and-you'll-miss-it town off Highway 400 (exit 153), just south of the Honey Harbour turnoff, but the town does have the nicest lodging in the vicinity of the national park.

If you want to stay somewhere a bit more lively, with more food and entertainment options, sleep in the Midland area and spend the day in the national park; it's about an hour's drive.

In Honey Harbour, the old-school **Delawana Inn Spa and Conference Resort** (42 Delawana Rd., 705/756-2424 or 800/627-3387, www.delawana.com, late May–mid-Oct.) has been operating its summer camp–like property since the 1890s, and it's the closest lodging to the national park. Sprawling over 10 hectares (25 acres), the family-friendly resort includes blocks of 120 motel-style rooms set amid broad lawns and evergreen trees. Some of the old-fashioned rooms could do with an upgrade, but with a pool, a beach, a nine-hole golf course, mini-golf, canoes, kayaks, and tennis courts, you won't lack for things to do. Boats shuttle guests to nearby Royal Island for hikes and nature programs, and in July and August, there are organized camp activities for kids and teens. Prices vary depending on the season, type of room, and the number of meals included; kids stay free during certain times. Nonguests can purchase a day pass to the resort for $30 per person. At the casual **Lake**

Country Grill (Nautilus Marina, 2755 Honey Harbour Rd., 705/756-0303, www.lakecountrygrill.com, May–mid-Oct., $9–20), which overlooks the water, pasta is a specialty, but you can also get pizza, burgers, and other pub fare. Or just have a beer while you watch the sunset.

In Port Severn, the **Rawley Resort and Spa** (2900 Kellys Rd., Port Severn, 705/538-2272 or 800/263-7538, www.rawleyresort.com) feels like a waterfront estate, particularly as you sit in the dining room, looking across the manicured lawns to the water. The restaurant feels quite formal, serving classic dishes such as veal scaloppini, grilled steak, or roasted Alaskan halibut, with live jazz several nights a week. Accommodations are spread over several buildings and range from upscale guest rooms, to large one- or two-bedroom suites, to two-story loft units overlooking the water. There's an outdoor pool, as well as a small beach.

CAMPING

Beausoleil Island has eight campgrounds. The largest is **Cedar Spring Campground** (705/526-8907, $25.50/site, reservation fee $9.80 per campsite), near the boat dock on the southeast side of the island, with 36 tent sites and four camping cabins, as well as flush toilets and showers.

The remaining primitive campgrounds ($15.70/site) are first-come, first-served with either pit or composting toilets. Payment is by self-registration permits available at each campground's docking area. Campers must bring their own water.

- **Honeymoon Bay** (13 sites), at the island's northernmost end
- **Chimney Bay** and **Oaks** (13 sites total)
- **Sandpiper** (eight sites)
- **Tonch North** (four sites)
- **Tonch East** (seven sites)
- **Tonch South** (seven sites)
- **Thumb Point** (eight sites)

Campers staying in the primitive areas can use the showers at Cedar Spring for a small fee. The park service also provides a drop-off and pickup service for campers staying in the primitive areas. Otherwise, if you arrive on the park service's *DayTripper* boat, which docks at Cedar Spring, you'll need to hike to your campsite. The walks to Christian Beach, Beausoleil Point, and Thumb Point campgrounds are under an hour; the others are much farther, so be prepared to carry your gear.

On several weekends in September and early October, the park service offers an **"All-Inclusive" Camping Experience** (705/526-8907, $299 for two adults, $179 for one adult, and $49 each child age 16 and under), handy for anyone who's new to camping or who doesn't want the hassle of assembling all the gear. Park staff will transport you to The Oaks, a seven-site camping area on a sheltered bay near the north end of Beausoleil Island. Staff provide comfortable, preassembled tents, with cots for the adults and sleeping pads for the kids, as well as drinking water, cooking equipment, camp chairs and table, a lantern, a canoe, and kayaks. They'll also cook your dinner on Friday night, but you'll need to bring your own sleeping bags and your food for the rest of the weekend. The all-inclusive weekend isn't a luxury experience—you'll still use an outhouse, and there are no shower facilities nearby—but a park staff person will be on-site to help throughout your stay.

Reservations are required, and because there are only seven campsites, it's a good idea to book early. Bookings are accepted beginning in April for the following autumn.

Information and Services

The administrative office of **Georgian Bay Islands National Park** (705/526-9804, email info.gbi@pc.gc.ca, 8 A.M.–4 P.M. Mon.–Fri.) is located in Midland. You can contact them for information by phone or email year-round.

The **Parks Canada Welcome Centre** (Port Severn, 705/538-2586, mid-May–mid-Oct) is just off Highway 400 (exit 153) between Midland and Honey Harbour. It's not in the national park, but they can give you information about park activities. The Welcome Centre is located at Lock 45 on the 386-kilometer

(240-mile) **Trent-Severn Waterway** that connects Lake Ontario with Georgian Bay; the lock station has a small exhibit area about the waterway and the lock system, and you can watch boats transiting the lock.

From mid-June until early September, the park service runs an **information kiosk** (8:30 A.M.–4 P.M. Sun.–Thurs., 8:30 A.M.–7:30 P.M. Fri.–Sat.) on Beausoleil Island, near the Cedar Spring Campground.

PARRY SOUND

Fronting Georgian Bay, Parry Sound is a jumping-off point for exploring the 30,000 Islands, which dot the waters just offshore. It's a popular destination for kayaking, whether you're just getting started or you're an experienced paddler. For a relatively small community (the year-round population is about 6,000), Parry Sound has a surprisingly robust cultural life, drawing music lovers in particular to the beautifully designed performing-arts center.

Parry Sound's most famous native son may be hockey player Bobby Orr, whose legacy lives on in the **Bobby Orr Hall of Fame** (Charles W. Stockey Centre for the Performing Arts, 2 Bay St., 705/746-4466 or 877/746-4466, www.bobbyorrhalloffame.com, 9 A.M.–5 P.M. Tues.–Sun. late June–early Sept., Wed.–Sat. early Sept.–late June; adults $9, seniors/children $6). The first-floor exhibits document Orr's legendary National Hockey League career, beginning in 1962, when the Boston Bruins recruited him for their junior team at age 14. If you have kids in tow, they'll likely head right to the second floor to play a variety of hockey skills games.

30,000 Islands Cruises

Off the Parry Sound coast, Georgian Bay is dotted with thousands of islands, and one of the best ways to explore this coastal region is on a cruise. The 550-passenger *Island Queen* (9 Bay St., 705/746-2311 or 800/506-2628, www.islandqueencruise.com), which bills itself as Canada's largest sightseeing boat, runs a three-hour cruise (1 P.M. daily, June–mid-Oct., adults $33, children 5–12 $16.50) that

passes by Killbear Provincial Park and circles a number of the islands. In July and August, there's also a two-hour morning cruise (10 A.M. daily, adults $25, children 5–12 $12.50) that sticks closer to shore and the inner islands, where you can catch glimpses of cottages and vacation homes.

After years of service as Niagara Falls' *Maid of the Mist*, the **M.V. *Chippewa III*** (Spirit of the Sound Schooner Company Ltd., Seguin River Parkette, off Bay St., 705/746-6064 or 888/283-5870, www.spiritofthesound.ca, July–Aug.) now tours the waters off Parry Sound. They offer a variety of island cruises, including a two-hour afternoon cruise (adults $24, children under 17 $12), a sunset cocktail cruise (adults $30, children under 17 $15), and a dinner cruise (adults $60, children under 15 $4 per year). They also run trips to **Henry's Fish Restaurant** on Frying Pan Island (adults $36, children under 17 $18), combining a cruise with a stop for a fish 'n' chips lunch.

🎬 Flight-Seeing

Touring the 30,000 Islands by boat is a lovely way to spend an afternoon, but seeing the islands by air is an entirely different thrill. Run by husband and wife pilots Keith and Nicole Saulnier, **Georgian Bay Airways** (11A Bay St., 705/774-9884 or 800/786-1704, www.georgianbayairways.com, May–Oct.) flies Cessna floatplanes that take off from Parry Sound Harbor and soar over the nearby islands.

Seeing the islands from above gives you a much clearer picture of both their number and their diversity. The chain of islands extends far across the horizon; some are barely more than a boulder in the bay, while others support entire towns. Keith and Nicole both know the region well, and can tell you all about the various islands as you circle.

The basic tour runs 25–35 minutes (adults $95–119), or you can opt for a variety of special flights, from a sunset champagne flight ($295 per couple) to a fish 'n' chips meal at Henry's Fish Restaurant (705/746-9040, mid-May–Sept., adults $159) on Frying Pan Island. They've hosted in-flight marriage proposals, and even a wedding, so if you have something special in mind, let them know.

Canoeing and Kayaking

The Parry Sound area is an excellent starting point for canoe or kayak tours, and one well-established local outfitter has two locations to help you get out on the water. The **White Squall Paddling Centre** (53 Carling Bay Rd., Nobel, 705/342-5324, www.whitesquall.com, 9 A.M.–5:30 P.M. daily Apr.–mid-Oct.), on Cole Lake, rents canoes and kayaks, offers lessons, and organizes a variety of day-trips, as well as multiday kayak tours. It's located off Highway 559 en route to Killbear Provincial Park.

In downtown Parry Sound, the **White Squall Outdoor Gear Store** (19 James St., 705/746-4936, www.whitesquall.com, 9:30 A.M.–5:30 P.M. Mon.–Sat., 11 A.M.–4 P.M. Sun.) is primarily a gear shop, but you can get information about their rentals and trips here, too. In July and August (Tues. 6:30–8 P.M.), they offer free kayaking and canoeing at Waubuno Beach (Prospect St.).

Entertainment and Shopping

The hub of cultural life in Parry Sound—indeed, in this entire region of Ontario—is the **Charles W. Stockey Centre for the Performing Arts** (2 Bay St., 705/746-4466 or 877/746-4466, www.stockeycentre.com). This striking contemporary building right on the bay, built of local timber and stone, hosts concerts, lectures, and other events year-round.

Parry Sound's major cultural event, held at the Stockey Centre, is the annual **Festival of the Sound** (42 James St., 705/746-2410 or 866/364-0061, www.festivalofthesound.ca). Since 1979, this classical-music festival has been drawing Canadian and international musicians—and music lovers—for three weeks of concerts in July and August.

Accommodations

Parry Sound has several B&Bs and small inns located between downtown and the harbor. If you're a porch lover, **Mariner's Rest Bed and Breakfast** (14 Belvedere Ave., 705/746-9011, www.bbcanada.com/8153.html, $80 s, $95 d), in a 1910 Arts and Crafts–style home, has two: a big front porch with wicker chairs for lounging and a screened-in porch for summer breakfasts. The two upstairs bedrooms are furnished with solid dark wood pieces and floral wallpaper. The house is on a residential street between downtown and the harbor.

Want more porch options? The nicest spots to relax at the homey **40 Bay Street Bed & Breakfast** (40 Bay St., 705/746-9247 or 866/371-2638, www.40baystreet.com, $125–140 d) are the two sunporches overlooking the harbor. The Bay Room, the smallest of the three cozy guest quarters (all with private baths), has expansive harbor views, too. The Retreat Room's special feature is the oversized bathroom, and the Garden Room lives up to its name with a private deck facing the flower-filled yard. Children under 11 are not permitted.

Built in 1882 (with a 1950s addition), the rambling 11-room **Bayside Inn** (10 Gibson St., 705/746-7720 or 866/833-8864, www.psbaysideinn.com, $128–143 d) is conveniently located near downtown. The rather ramshackle exterior belies the well-turned-out rooms, done in a modern country style, that all have air-conditioning, flat-screen TVs, wireless Internet, and refrigerators. Unlike many small inns, the family-owned Bayside welcomes families; ask for a room with two sleeping areas separated by a divider. Free coffee and tea are available every morning, and guests can have breakfast for a small additional charge (continental $4, full breakfast $8).

Though rustic on the outside, the six units (in three cabins) at the **Log Cabin Inn** (9 Lil Beaver Blvd. at Oastler Park Dr., 705/746-7122, www.logcabininn.net, $150 d) are country-contemporary inside, with a king or two queen beds, fireplaces, and modern baths. Rooms overlook the river, and while not plush by city standards, they'd make a comfortable spot for a getaway. Rates include continental breakfast, and packages including breakfast and dinner in the upscale restaurant are available. The property is three kilometers (1.9 miles) south of town.

Food

The downtown area, around the intersection of Seguin and James Streets, has several basic places to eat. Along the harbor, Bay Street has a couple of seasonal eateries, open only in the summer.

The stacks of newspapers (plus books for the kids) encourage lingering at **Hanson's Mad Hatter Café** (35 Seguin St., 705/746-8992, www.hansonsmadhatter.com, 7 A.M.–4 P.M. Mon.–Fri., 8:30 A.M.–4 P.M. Sat.), where you can stop in for coffee and muffins, settle in for lunch, or pick up a sandwich to go. Roast beef, chicken, and bacon all figure prominently among the sandwiches, but several options, like the avocado-veggie wrap, are vegetarian-friendly.

Families and couples, tourists and locals, even the occasional visiting hockey team all turn up at **Wellington's Pub and Grill** (105 James St., 705/746-1333, $9–19), a friendly pub-restaurant downtown decorated with black-and-white photos from Parry Sound's past. From salads to steaks to schnitzel, the food is decent enough (you can't go wrong with the bacon-topped chicken sandwich), and the bar stocks plenty of local brews; you also get free Wi-Fi.

For more gourmet dining, head south of town to the **Log Cabin Inn** (9 Lil Beaver Blvd. at Oastler Park Dr., 705/746-7122, www.log-cabininn.net, lunch $8–15, dinner $20–40), where you can sample grilled elk chops, pan-seared rainbow trout, or roast chicken in, yes, a log cabin. Don't expect pioneer hardship, though; the solid log structure with a soaring ceiling overlooks the river, with a fireplace, twinkling candles, and a lengthy wine list setting the mood.

Practicalities

Georgian Bay Country Tourism (1A Church St., 705/746-4455 or 888/746-4455, www.gb-country.com) can provide information about the Parry Sound region. If you're heading toward Parry Sound from the south, stop into their **Georgian Bay Country Visitor Centre** (1 Horseshoe Lake Rd., 705/378-5105 or 888/229-7257) at Exit 214 off Highway 400/69.

The **Rainbow Country Travel Association** (2726 Whippoorwill Ave., Sudbury, 705/522-0104 or 800/465-6655, www.rainbowcountry.com) is another source of information about Parry Sound.

Parry Sound is 222 kilometers (138 miles) northwest of Toronto along Highway 400/69. It's 163 kilometers (105 miles) south of Sudbury via Highway 69. **Ontario Northland** (800/461-8558, www.ontarionorthland.ca) runs buses to Parry Sound from Toronto and Sudbury. There are two buses daily in each direction between Toronto and Parry Sound (3.5 hours, adults $53) and between Parry Sound and Sudbury (2 hours, adults $37). Buses stop at Richard's Coffee (119 Bowes St., 705/746-9611), about 1.8 kilometers (1.1 miles) east of downtown.

Three times a week, the VIA Rail *Canadian* between Vancouver and Toronto stops at **Parry Sound Train Station** (70 Church St., 888/842-7245, www.viarail.ca), about one kilometer (0.6 mile) north of downtown, but the schedule is much less convenient than the bus.

Parry Sound's attractions are clustered along the harbor, which is a short walk from downtown. The town has no public transit, so if you don't have a car, choose a lodging near the harbor or downtown and take a cab from the station to your accommodations. You can then walk to attractions and restaurants. For taxi service, try **Parry Sound Taxi** (705/746-1221).

◖ KILLBEAR PROVINCIAL PARK

With pink granite cliffs, windblown pines, and several long sandy beaches along Georgian Bay, Killbear Provincial Park (35 Killbear Park Rd., Nobel, 705/342-5492, www.ontarioparks.com, $13/vehicle) is a spectacular location for outdoor activities, from hiking to canoeing to swimming. Lesser known than Ontario's "destination" provincial parks like Algonquin or Killarney, Killbear is less than an hour's drive from Parry Sound, which makes it an easy day trip. If you'd like to stay longer, Killbear's campgrounds are the third largest in the Ontario provincial park system (only Algonquin and The Pinery have more campsites).

The park **Visitor Centre** (705/342-5492, 10 a.m.–5 p.m. daily mid-May–mid-Oct.) has a variety of exhibits about the geology, natural history, and cultural history of the Killbear area. Particularly popular with the kids (well, with most of them) are the snake exhibits; in summer, naturalists give "snake talks" where you can learn about and touch local reptiles. In July and August, you can join in a daily interpretive program; there are guided hikes, slide shows, kids' activities, and more. And be sure to walk around to the back of the Visitor Centre for great views of Georgian Bay.

Killbear is home to the endangered Massasuaga rattlesnake. While it's not likely you'll see one, if you do come upon a rattlesnake near the campgrounds or along the road, notify a park staff person, who will relocate the snake to a less-traveled area. Don't try to pick up or move the snake yourself.

The park is officially open mid-May through mid-October, but in the off-season, you can walk in for winter hiking, cross-country skiing, or snowshoeing.

Sports and Recreation

Several easy hiking trails wend through the park, making Killbear good for novice hikers. Heading along the shoreline out to the far end of the park, the **Lighthouse Point Trail** is an easy one-kilometer (0.6-mile) route that passes a 1904 lighthouse. The 3.5-kilometer (2.2-mile) **Lookout Point Trail** goes through the forest to a lookout above Georgian Bay. For the bayside views of the park's pink granite rocks, follow the **Twin Points Trail,** a 1.5-kilometer (0.9-mile) path loop from the day-use parking area. A six-kilometer (3.7-mile) walking and cycling trail runs from the park entrance past several of the campgrounds to Lighthouse Point.

Killbear's three kilometers (1.9 miles) of sandy beaches include a popular swimming beach at the day-use area. You can swim near most of the campgrounds, as well. **Harold**

Point, with both a sand beach and rocky cliffs, is a pretty spot to watch the sunset.

Surrounded by water on three sides, Killbear is a popular destination for canoeing and kayaking. The most sheltered waters are near the park's day-use area. Canoe and kayak rentals are not available inside the park, but you can rent boats from nearby outfitters (mid-May–mid-Oct.). **Killbear Park Mall** (Hwy. 559, Nobel, 705/342-5747, www.killbearparkmall.com), a general store and gear-rental shop just outside the park entrance, rents canoes ($23/day), single kayaks ($29/day), and double kayaks ($45/day). Located four kilometers (2.5 miles) east of the park, **The Detour Store** (401 Hwy. 559, Nobel, 705/342-1611, www.thedetourstore.ca) rents canoes ($20–22/day) and kayaks ($20–35/day single, $40/day double), too. **White Squall Paddling Centre** (53 Carling Bay Rd., Nobel, 705/342-5324, www.whitesquall.com), located off Highway 559 en route to Killbear, also rents a variety of different types of canoes ($28–38/day) and kayaks ($22–45/day single, $30–65/day double). White Squall has a shuttle service to deliver boats to various locations in and around the park.

Camping

Killbear Provincial Park (35 Killbear Park Rd., Nobel, 705/342-5492, www.ontarioparks.com, $34.25 tent sites, $37.75 premium sites, $39.25 sites with electrical service) has seven different campgrounds, with a total of 880 campsites, most within a five-minute walk of the shore. All the campgrounds, except for the more remote, 55-site Granite Saddle area, have restrooms, showers, and laundry facilities. About a quarter of the sites have electrical hookups.

Among the prime sites are the waterfront campsites fronting the beach at **Kilcoursie Bay.** Other campgrounds with waterfront sites include **Beaver Dams, Harold Point,** and **Lighthouse Point.**

Killbear's campgrounds are exceedingly popular, and they book up early, so make reservations (Ontario Parks Reservation Service, 888/668-7275, www.ontarioparks.com, reservation fees $8.50 online, $9.50 by phone) well in advance. You can make reservations up to five months before your stay.

Practicalities

Contact the **Killbear Provincial Park office** (35 Killbear Park Rd., Nobel, 705/342-5492, www.ontarioparks.com) or check online (Friends of Killbear, www.friendsofkillbear. com) for more information. Several small stores along Highway 559 stock food and other provisions. For a better selection, do your shopping in Parry Sound.

By road, Killbear Provincial Park is 35 kilometers (22 miles) northwest of Parry Sound, about a 45-minute drive. From Parry Sound, take Highway 69 north to Nobel, where you pick up Highway 559 west to the park. There's no public transportation to or around the park, so you'll need to come by car.

Muskoka Cottage Country

With more lakes than you can count, the Muskoka region is one of Ontario's vacation lands. For many Ontarians, Muskoka is "Cottage Country," a place to escape from the city's frenzy, where your obligations are nothing more than to sit on the porch of your summer cottage and relax. Even people who don't have cottages of their own (or friends with cottages who invite them for weekends) head to Cottage Country, to stay in B&Bs, hotels, or the many cottage resorts that still dot the lakes.

The Muskoka region, north of Toronto, encompasses the towns of Gravenhurst, Bracebridge, and Huntsville, among others, extending northwest to Georgian Bay and northeast to Algonquin Provincial Park. Tourism to Muskoka began in earnest in the 1800s when steamboats transported visitors across the lakes. These days, nearly all the steamboats are gone (except for a couple used for sightseeing cruises), but the tourists continue to come. And if you're looking for a place to get outdoors, whether to hike, canoe, or just sit on the porch, you should, too.

BARRIE

Barrie isn't really part of the Muskoka region, but you'll likely pass through the city on your way north. Even though it's 105 kilometers (65 miles) north of Toronto, it feels like an extension of the metropolitan area (and people do commute daily from Barrie to Toronto), rather than the start of a cottage holiday. Still, it's a handy spot to break up your drive, whether to have a bite to eat or to stay for a day or two. And if you're continuing north from Barrie, stop in the town of Orillia to tour the former home of noted Canadian humorist Stephen Leacock.

Barrie spreads out along the shore of Lake Simcoe, so even in the heart of the city, you can stroll along the lake. Dunlop Street is the main downtown thoroughfare; most sights and shops are on or around Dunlop.

Barrie has a small but worthwhile art museum, the **Maclaren Art Centre** (37 Mulcaster St., 705/721-9696, www.maclarenart.com, 10 A.M.–5 P.M. Mon.–Fri., 10 A.M.–4 P.M. Sat., noon–4 P.M. Sun., adults $5), which exhibits work by established Canadian and emerging regional artists. Half of the building was Barrie's original public library, built in 1917; the other half is an airy contemporary addition built in 2001. In the main lobby, look for the door that designer and goldsmith Donald A. Stuart reworked into a multimedia art installation, bejeweled with drawing pencils, rulers, rocks, and luminous slabs of wood. If you're looking for a gift for an arty friend, browse the jewelry and works by local artists in the gallery shop.

You can cruise the lake on the *Serendipity Princess* (Bayfield St., at Simcoe St., 705/728-9888, www.midlandtours.com, June–Sept., adults $25, seniors $23, students $20, kids $5–14, families $67), a paddle-wheel boat that offers daily summer sightseeing excursions. Boats depart from the Barrie Town Dock.

If you're heading north and need outdoor gear, Barrie has an outpost of the massive **Mountain Equipment Co-op** (61 Bryne Dr., 705/792-4675, www.mec.ca, 10 A.M.–7 P.M. Mon.–Wed., 10 A.M.–9 P.M. Thurs.–Fri., 9 A.M.–6 P.M. Sat., 11 A.M.–5 P.M. Sun.), a Canadian chain that stocks clothing, camping equipment, cycling gear, and other supplies for outdoor adventures. You must be a member to make a purchase, but anyone can join simply by paying the $5 lifetime membership fee. The Barrie store is just off Highway 400 (exit 94, Essa Rd.).

Accommodations

Several chain motels cluster along Hart Drive (take the Dunlop Street exit off Highway 400), in an area that has nothing much to recommend it except views of the highway. Closer to downtown, you'll find more appealing B&Bs and small inns.

Owners Pam and Bob Richmond have set up a separate wing for guests on the second floor of their 1911 brick Georgian-style home east of downtown. The **Richmond Manor B&B** (16 Blake St., 705/726-7103, www.bbcanada.com/1145.html, $75–100 d) has two large, traditionally furnished guest rooms with peek-a-boo views of Kempenfelt Bay. A shared bath is located between the rooms, and across the hall is a guest lounge with a TV/DVD player. Breakfast is a formal affair, served on fine china in the stately dining room.

Catering to business travelers and people relocating to the Barrie area, the **Harbour View Inn** (1 Berczy St., 705/735-6832, www.harbourviewinn.ca, $129–349) has eight rooms and suites—some with lake views— in a brick Victorian just east of downtown. While the accommodations aren't large, they all have kitchenettes, with a microwave, a mini-fridge, a coffeemaker, a toaster, and dishes; some have sleep sofas to accommodate an extra guest. Free Wi-Fi.

Food

One of Ontario's largest and longest running farmers' markets, the year-round **Barrie Farmers' Market** (Collier St. at Mulcaster St., www.barriefarmermarket.com, 8 A.M.–noon Sat.) has been operating since 1846. You can buy seasonal produce, prepared foods, baked goods (mmm, butter tarts), and crafts. From May to October, the market is outside on the plaza in front of City Hall; from November to April, it moves inside the City Hall building.

Some of Barrie's most interesting food isn't in the downtown area—it's in the strip malls and industrial parks off Highway 400. A good example is **Cravings Fine Food** (131 Commerce Park Dr., 705/734-2272, www.cravingsfinefood.ca, 9 A.M.–6 P.M. Mon.–Tues., 9 A.M.–7 P.M. Wed.–Fri., 9 A.M.–5 P.M. Sun.), a café and gourmet shop that sells beautifully crafted (and scrumptious) pastries, sandwiches, salads, and other prepared foods, perfect for a quick meal on the road or to take north to the cottage.

If you love butter tarts (and who doesn't?), find your way to the strip mall that houses **The Sweet Oven** (75 Barrie View Dr., #103A, 705/733-9494, www.thesweetoven.com, 10 A.M.–6 P.M. Mon.–Sat.), which makes these tasty tarts ($2, or $10 for six) in numerous varieties. Flavors like peanut butter, mint, or chai are novelties, but the classics—plain, pecan, or raisin—are the best.

Barbecue tastes best when you have to hunt for it in an out-of-the-way locale, doesn't it? At least it does at the **Big Chris BBQ Smokehouse** (110 Anne St., #8, 705/721-7427, www.bigchrisbbq.ca, 11 A.M.–11 P.M. daily, $8–20) in an industrial park between Highway 400 and downtown. The Texas-sized portions of ribs, pulled pork, and burgers come with cole slaw, baked beans, and a heap of French fries. If the flavors are more mild-mannered Canadian than Texas badass, just add some hot sauce and dig in. The interior is about as charming as a fast-food franchise, but service is nearly as speedy.

Information and Services

You can pick up all sorts of information about Barrie and the surrounding region at the helpful **Tourism Barrie Visitor Information**

Centre (205 Lakeshore Dr., 705/739-9444 or 800/668-9100, www.tourismbarrie.com, 9 A.M.–5 P.M. Mon.–Fri., 10 A.M.–4 P.M. Sat.), located on the south side of Lake Simcoe. In July and August, they're also open Sunday (10 A.M.–4 P.M.). Tourism Barrie also staffs a seasonal **Downtown Information Kiosk** (Bayfield St. at Simcoe St., 9 A.M.–7 P.M. daily May–mid-Oct.).

The provincially run **Ontario Travel Information Centre** (21 Mapleview Dr. E., 705/725-7280 or 800/567-1140, www.ontariotravel.net, 8 A.M.–8 P.M. daily June–Aug., 8:30 A.M.–4:30 P.M. daily Sept.–May), just off Highway 400, can help with travel questions about Barrie and points north.

Getting There and Around

Both **Ontario Northland** (800/461-8558, www.ontarionorthland.ca, adults $22 one-way) and **Greyhound Bus Lines** (800/661-8747, www.greyhound.ca, adults $19–28 one-way) stop at the Barrie Bus Terminal (24 Maple Ave., 705/739-1500) downtown. Between Barrie and Toronto, there are frequent buses throughout the day in both directions; it's about a 90-minute trip. Ontario Northland buses continue north from Barrie to Gravenhurst, Bracebridge, Huntsville, and North Bay; another travels toward Parry Sound and Sudbury.

Simcoe County Airport Service (137 Brock St., 705/728-1148 or 800/461-7529, www.simcoecountyairportservice.ca, one-way $62/person, $87/two, $111/three, $134/four) runs door-to-door van service from Toronto's Pearson airport to Barrie. Book online or by phone.

Barrie Transit (705/739-4209, www.barrie.ca, $2.75/ride), the city's bus service, can take you around town if you don't have a car. Get a transfer when you board, since it's good for 60 minutes (even if you're heading back in the same direction), and parents, take note: up to three elementary school kids ride free with a paying adult.

If you're heading farther north from Barrie, you can rent a car here, which may be less expensive than picking up a rental in Toronto. Many car rental companies have Barrie offices, including **Avis** (425 Dunlop St. W., 705/726-6527 or 800/879-2847, www.avis.com), **Budget** (520 Bryne Dr., #10, 705/737-0333 or 800/268-8900, www.budget.ca), **Discount Car Rentals** (15 George St., 705/722-8900, www.discount-car.com), and **Enterprise Rent-A-Car** (304 Dunlop St. W., Unit 4, 705/728-1212 or 800/736-8222, www.enterpriserentacar.ca).

ORILLIA

Though his "day job" was as a political science professor at Montreal's McGill University, Stephen Leacock (1869–1944) became famous as a writer and humorist. He published 35 humor books over his career, including *Sunshine Sketches of a Little Town* (1912) and *Arcadian Adventures of the Idle Rich* (1914).

In 1928, Leacock built a summer house near Old Brewery Bay in the town of Orillia. The home became his permanent residence following his retirement from McGill in 1936 until his death 12 years later. It is now the **Stephen Leacock Museum** (50 Museum Dr., Orillia, 705/329-1908, www.leacockmuseum.com, 9 A.M.–5 P.M. daily June–Sept., 9 A.M.–5 P.M. Mon.–Fri. Oct.–May, adults $5, seniors $4, students $3, kids $2). Some parts of the house are (nearly) as Leacock left them, including the sunroom with his work table, his study, and his living room facing the lake. On the main floor are signed original portraits of Leacock that noted photographer Yousuf Karsh took at the home in 1941.

Orillia is 40 kilometers (25 miles) northeast of Barrie. Go north on Highway 11 to Highway 12, then turn left on Atherley Road and follow the signs to the museum.

GRAVENHURST

You know you've arrived in Cottage Country when you pass by the **world's largest Muskoka chair** (1170 Muskoka Rd. S.), located outside the Gravenhurst Home Hardware store at the south end of town. What's a "Muskoka chair," you may ask? It's the laid-back wooden porch chair that most Americans call an Adirondack chair. This symbol of relaxation gives you a clue of what Gravenhurst is all about.

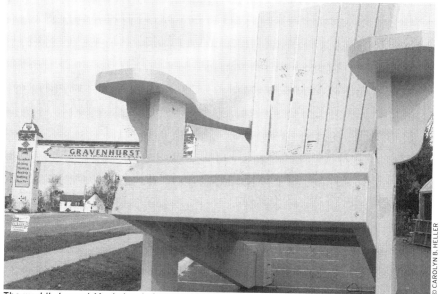

The world's largest Muskoka chair welcomes visitors to Gravenhurst.

© CAROLYN B. HELLER

Gravenhurst's main attractions are at Muskoka Wharf (www.muskokawharf.ca), the lakefront development where you can tour a boat museum or cruise the lake in a traditional steamship. The town is also the birthplace of Norman Bethune, a Canadian doctor who became wildly famous in China, where he's still considered a hero long after his death.

Gravenhurst Opera House (295 Muskoka Rd. S., 705/687-5550 or 888/495-8888, www.gravenhurstoperahouse.com), built in 1901, now hosts concerts, plays, and films. **Music on the Barge** (Gull Lake Rotary Park, Brock St., at Bethune Dr., 7:30 P.M. Sun. mid-June–mid-Aug.) has brought toe-tapping summer concerts, from big band to Dixieland to folk, to the waterfront since 1959.

Muskoka Wharf

The Muskoka Lakes Navigation Company opened in 1866 and during its heyday operated the largest fleet of inland lake steamships in North America. The ships carried both passengers and freight across the Muskoka Lakes, providing service where the railroads didn't reach and roads either didn't go or were difficult to navigate. At one time, there were more than 100 lakeside hotels in the Muskokas whose guests all arrived by steamship.

One of these ships, the **R.M.S. Segwun,** was built in 1887 and used as an official "Royal Mail Ship." Today, it's North America's oldest operating steamship. **Muskoka Steamships** (185 Cherokee Ln., 705/687-6667 or 866/687-6667, www.segwun.com, mid-June–mid-Oct.) offers a variety of sightseeing cruises on the *Segwun,* departing from their Muskoka Wharf docks. The schedules vary with the seasons, but you can choose from 1–4-hour trips (adults $17.95–48.95, kids $10.95–34.95).

Back on land, explore the region's steamship traditions at the **Muskoka Boat and Heritage Centre** (275 Steamship Bay Rd., 705/687-2115, www.realmuskoka.com, 10 A.M.–6 P.M. Tues.–Fri., 10 A.M.–4 P.M. Sat.–Mon. summer; 10 A.M.–4 P.M. Tues.–Sat. winter; adults $7.50, seniors $5.50, kids $3.50, families $18.50), a creatively designed museum, filled with multimedia exhibits. One section of the museum is a re-created lakeside hotel, where the owner welcomes you (in a video) when you enter the lobby and you can pretend that you're holidaying in the 19th century. Another exhibit is a re-created steamship that you can go aboard. You can also visit the Grace and Speed Boathouse, North America's only in-water exhibit of working antique boats, with up to 20 spiffy craft on view.

Bethune Memorial House National Historic Site

Born in Gravenhurst, Henry Norman Bethune (1890–1939) became a legendary physician, known largely for a brief tour of service on the other side of the world. Bethune was a surgeon, working in Montreal during the Depression of the 1930s. Not only did he develop new surgical techniques and devices (one of these inventions, the Bethune rib shears, is still used today), he was also something of a radical, becoming an early advocate for socialized medicine in Canada. He joined the Communist Party in 1936.

In 1938, after China and Japan went to war, Bethune decided to travel to China to tend to the injured. Arriving at the front, he was appalled to discover that the Chinese had few trained medical personnel. He implemented a medical education program and established mobile medical facilities, including an operating theater that two mules could carry. The legend of the foreign doctor's commitment to the Chinese began to spread across China. After spending less than two years in the country, however, Bethune accidentally cut his finger while performing an operation. He developed a particularly aggressive form of blood poisoning, which killed him within the month. Chinese leader Mao Tse-tung wrote an essay, "In Memory of Norman Bethune," which became required reading for Chinese students and helped solidify Bethune's memory.

The Bethune Memorial House National Historic Site (297 John St. N., 705/687-4261, www.pc.gc.ca, 10 A.M.–4 P.M. daily June–Oct., adults $3.90, seniors $3.40, kids 6–16 $1.90,

families $9.80) consists of two buildings: one is a museum that recounts Bethune's history; the other is the 1880 home next door where Bethune was born. Bethune lived in the house only a short time, so most of the contents are from the period rather than the family.

Try to visit on a weekday if you can, when the house's diminutive rooms are less crowded and staff have more time to tell you about Bethune's legacy.

Tree Museum

One of Cottage Country's most offbeat attractions is this outdoor art gallery outside of Gravenhurst. No, the Tree Museum (1634 Doe Lake Rd., 705/684-8185, www.thetreemuseum.ca, dawn–dusk daily, free) isn't a museum of trees—it's a gallery set outside in the woods. As you wander along the hiking trails through the 80-hectare (200-acre) woodland, spy imaginative sculptures and other eclectic works set among the trees. Be prepared for a lot of walking along the sometimes muddy paths. It's one kilometer (0.6 mile) from the parking area to the first sculpture, and another 1.2 kilometers (0.75 mile) to the center of the site; return the way you came. The museum has no restrooms or other facilities, so bring some water and a snack.

To get to the Tree Museum, follow Highway 11 north past Gravenhurst, then exit at Doe Lake Road (Muskoka Road 6). Go east about eight kilometers (five miles) farther till you see museum signs on your right.

Accommodations

The **Residence Inn by Marriott** (285 Steamship Bay Rd, Muskoka Wharf, 705/687-6600 or 866/580-6238, www.marriott.com, $165–399 d) is located at Muskoka Wharf, overlooking Lake Muskoka. The 106 modern suites all have kitchen facilities and include studios with sleeper sofas and larger units with one or two bedrooms. Rates include a buffet breakfast, parking, and Internet access.

In the woods on Lake Muskoka north of town, the expansive (and expensive) **Taboo Resort** (1209 Muskoka Beach Rd., 705/687-2233 or 800/461-0236, www.tabooresort.com, mid-Feb.–Oct., $299–639 d) feels like two resorts in one. Some of the 101 guest rooms have a traditional Muskoka feel, with overstuffed chairs and wooden cottage-style furniture, while others are sleek and modern, all satiny woods and chrome; the best rooms of both types are right above the lake. Thirty condos, ranging from two to four bedrooms, are scattered around the property; they're individually decorated, giving them each a distinct personality, although most don't have lake views. You won't be bored here, with a private beach, three outdoor pools, an indoor pool, and one pool just for the kids, plus golf, a spa, two restaurants, and a poolside bar. Expect to pay a resort fee that covers various activities, including the use of canoes and kayaks.

Food

Though it looks a bit twee, with its floral café curtains and blue-and-white china, the **Blue Willow Tea Shop** (900 Bay St., Muskoka Wharf, 705/687-2597, www.bluewillowteashop.ca, 11 A.M.–3 P.M. Tues.–Thurs., 11 A.M.–8 P.M. Fri.–Sat., $7–14) overlooks the lake and makes a good rest stop while visiting Muskoka Wharf. They serve soups, salads, and sandwiches at lunch, along with a large selection of black, green, and fruit teas. Midafternoon, you can take a tea break with a scone, a tart, or a slice of cake, or settle in for a traditional high tea.

Hip, urban **North Restaurant and Lounge** (530 Muskoka Road N., 705/687-8618, www.northinmuskoka.com, Apr.–Dec., call for seasonal hours, lunch $9–16, dinner $20–40) would be right at home in the big city, with its contemporary decor and dishes. Lunch runs from sandwiches—like glazed ham, Brie, and arugula served with lemon-apple slaw on raisin bread—to traditional eggs Benedict to a hearty plate of spaghetti with homemade meatballs. In the evening, choices might include roast Cornish hen with root veggies or beer-braised bison short ribs. If you want a bite to go, come around back to the **Back Door Fish with Chips** ($7–15), their to-go fish shack.

Information and Services

Muskoka Tourism (800/267-9700, www.muskokatourism.ca) provides information about the entire Muskoka Lakes region, including the Gravenhurst area. They operate a travel information center on Highway 11 south of Gravenhurst in the town of Kilworthy. The **Gravenhurst Chamber of Commerce** (685-2 Muskoka Rd. N., 705/687-4432, www.gravenhurstchamber.com, 8:30 A.M.–4:30 P.M. Mon.–Fri.) publishes an annual visitors' guide, with details on attractions, accommodations, restaurants, and events. It's available online or from their office.

Getting There and Around

Gravenhurst is 180 kilometers (112 miles) north of Toronto and 75 kilometers (47 miles) north of Barrie. From Toronto, pick up Highway 400 north to Barrie, then continue north on Highway 11 into Gravenhurst.

Ontario Northland trains and buses both stop at **Gravenhurst Station** (150 Second St. S., 705/687-2301 or 800/461-8558, www.ontarionorthland.ca, 2–2.5 hours, one-way adults $36.45, seniors and students $31, kids 2–11 $18.20) en route from Toronto's Union Station.

Shuttle Ontario (317 Carmichael Dr., North Bay, 705/474-7942 or 800/461-4219, www.shuttleontario.com, 2 hours, one-way adults $83) makes two scheduled trips a day in each direction between Toronto's Pearson Airport and Gravenhurst.

Exploring Gravenhurst is easiest if you have a car, although you can walk between Muskoka Wharf and the town center. **Discount Car Rentals** (1011 Airport Rd., 705/645-4878, www.discountcar.com) is located between Gravenhurst and Bracebridge. **Enterprise Rent-A-Car** (800/736-8222, www.enterpriserentacar.ca) has an office in Bracebridge.

BRACEBRIDGE

Like many Muskoka towns, Bracebridge's tourism industry goes back to the late 1800s, when visitors from Toronto came to the region by train and boat. Most of the old-time resorts are gone, but the town's main street, Manitoba Street, has an old-timey feel that makes for a pleasant stroll. Bracebridge is a good base for exploring the region—it's an easy drive to Gravenhurst or Huntsville and to other towns dotting the surrounding lakes—and with comfortable B&Bs and excellent restaurants, it's also a spot where you can just unwind.

Since the "lakes" are an important part of the Muskoka Lakes experience, get yourself out on the water. One option is to head out with **Lady Muskoka Cruises** (300 Ecclestone Dr., 705/646-2628 or 800/263-5239, www.ladymuskoka.com, late May–mid-Oct.), which operates sightseeing boats on Lake Muskoka. Cruises run at noon daily in July and August; in May and June and in September and October, there are noontime cruises on Saturdays, Sundays, and (except in May) on Wednesdays.

Bracebridge's own microbrewery, **Muskoka Brewery** (13 Taylor Rd., 705/646-1266, www.muskokabrewery.com), welcomes visitors to their shop, where they'll share their enthusiasm for beer brewing and maybe give you a taste or two.

A Bracebridge summer tradition is the free **Bandshell Concert Series** (Memorial Park, Manitoba St., www.bracebridge.ca) on Thursday evenings from June through early September.

Accommodations

Sandy Yudin has run **Century House B&B** (155 Dill St., 705/645-9903, www.bbmuskoka.com/centuryhouse, $60–70 s, $80–90 d), the 1855 brick farmhouse she shares with her husband Norman Yan, for nearly two decades, and she knows how to make guests feel at home. Sandy is warm and chatty, offering restaurant suggestions and ideas of things to do. The simple, traditional B&B rooms are furnished with quilts, wicker chairs, and antiques and have all the essentials—comfortable beds, reading lamps, bathrobes—but no extraneous frills. Located on the second floor, the three guest rooms share two baths. Sandy's a great cook, too, serving multicourse breakfasts with fresh fruit, eggs, smoked trout, and toast with homemade jams (mmm, tangy peach marmalade).

The B&B is in a residential neighborhood about a 15-minute walk from the shops and restaurants on Manitoba Street.

Although it's just a short walk from the town center, the **Bay House Bed and Breakfast** (2 Dominion St., 705/645-7508, www.bbmuskoka.com/bayhouse, $128–168) feels like a cottage in the woods. The three guest rooms are on the lower level, done in cheery pastel colors. The largest, the Bay Suite, has an electric fireplace and four-poster bed, while the Garden Room opens onto the patio. Jan and Peter Rickard are experienced innkeepers who are full of tips for things to do, although after their hearty breakfasts (which might include lemon ricotta pancakes or eggs hollandaise), you may be tempted just to soak in the outdoor hot tub.

Food

You can have a sandwich at **Marty's "World Famous" Café** (5 Manitoba St., 705/645-4794, www.martysworldfamous.com), but the shop's self-proclaimed fame is for the gooey, caramel butter tarts. Though some might bridle at the in-your-face self-promotion (and the excessively runny tart filling), no one disputes their advice not to eat these runny pastries in your car, or, as they warn, "You'll end up wearing them!"

A friendly joint for hanging out and having a an interesting microbrew, **The Griffin Gastropub** (9 Chancery Ln., 705/646-0438, www.thegriffinpub.ca, noon–midnight Tues.–Wed., noon–2 A.M. Thurs.–Sat., $8–13) also serves inventive pub grub, from addictive risotto balls to bison burgers to sticky toffee pudding. They usually have live folk, rock, blues, or jazz starting around 9 P.M. Thursday through Saturday. The pub is at the top of a narrow alleyway, off Manitoba Street.

Don't be put off by the strip mall setting behind the Tim Hortons. There's some serious sushi savvy in this chic Japanese restaurant. At **Wabora Fusion Japanese Restaurant** (295 Wellington St., #17, 705/646-9500, www.waborasushi.com, 11 A.M.–11 P.M. daily, $5–15), the cavernous room has a bar at one end, with

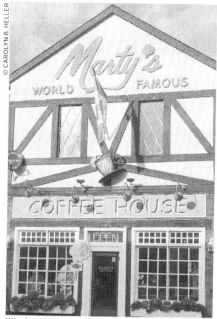

© CAROLYN B. HELLER

What's Marty famous for? Butter tarts!

artfully arranged bottles, and a well-lit sushi bar where the chefs ply their trade. The specialties on the huge menu are the wildly imaginative *maki* rolls, like the Bracebridge (salmon, crab, asparagus, and gobo wrapped in cucumber with lemon-ponzu-caramel sauce) or the Spicy Cottage (shrimp tempura, crab, spicy tuna, greens, cucumber, mango, and avocado in a rice paper roll with creamy wasabi sauce), but the straight-up *nigiri* is first-rate, too. If it's your birthday, they'll ring a gong and serenade you.

Colorful original artwork seems to pop out from the white walls at **One Fifty Five** (155 Manitoba St., 705/645-1935, lunch 11:30 A.M.–2:30 P.M. Tues–Sat., dinner 5–9:30 P.M. Tues–Sun., lunch $11–16, dinner $18–36), Bracebridge's white-tablecloth restaurant. The menu is colorful, too, with choices like chicken stuffed with Oka cheese from Quebec or panko-crusted pickerel. For dessert, it's hard to choose between the warm chocolate tart or the "zesty" lemon tart topped with fresh berries.

Information and Services

Tourism Bracebridge (1 Manitoba St., 705/645-8121 or 866/645-8121, www.tourism-bracebridge.com) provides information about the area, including an annual visitors' guide listing special events.

Getting There and Around

Bracebridge is 195 kilometers (121 miles) north of Toronto and 18 kilometers (11 miles) north of Gravenhurst. From Toronto, pick up Highway 400 north to Barrie, then continue north on Highway 11 to Bracebridge.

Ontario Northland (800/461-8558, www.ontarionorthland.ca, 2.5 hours, one-way adults $39.30, seniors and students, $33.40, kids 2–11 $19.65) runs the daily *Northlander* train from Toronto's Union Station to the **Bracebridge train station** (88 Hiram St.), right downtown. Ontario Northland buses stop at the Riverside Inn (300 Ecclestone Dr., 705/646-2239 or 800/461-8558, www.ontarionorthland.ca), south of downtown. From Toronto, bus fares are the same as the train fares. Both buses and trains continue to Huntsville, North Bay, Temagami, and points farther north.

Shuttle Ontario (317 Carmichael Dr., North Bay, 705/474-7942 or 800/461-4219, www.shuttleontario.com, 2.25 hours, one-way adults $85) makes two scheduled trips a day in each direction between Toronto's Pearson airport and Bracebridge.

Bracebridge is fairly small and compact, so you could arrive by train or bus and amuse yourself in town without a car. If you want to use Bracebridge as a base to explore the Muskoka region, though, you need to have your own vehicle. Car rental companies with Bracebridge offices include **Enterprise Rent-A-Car** (1 Armstrong St., 705/645-5952 or 800/736-8222, www.enterpriserentacar.ca) and **Discount Car Rentals** (15 Keith Rd., 705/645-4878, www.discountcar.com).

Huntsville and Vicinity

Located just west of Algonquin Provincial Park, the attractive town of Huntsville is a favorite destination in its own right, with lots of outdoor activities, good places to eat, and a cute downtown. But it's also close enough to Algonquin that you can easily stay in town and make day trips into the park.

SIGHTS

Start your Huntsville visit walking around downtown, looking for the colorful wall murals that decorate the town buildings. The murals constitute the **Group of Seven Outdoor Gallery** (www.groupofsevenoutdoorgallery.ca); they're replicas of works by the artists from the "Group of Seven" who worked in Ontario in the early 1900s. To do a complete mural tour, pick up a brochure from the **Huntsville/Lake of Bays Chamber of Commerce** (8 West St. N., 705/789-4771, www. huntsvilleadventures.com).

Muskoka Heritage Place

If you're interested in the history and development of the Muskoka region, there's lots to see and do at Muskoka Heritage Place (88 Brunel Rd., 705/789-7576, www.muskokaheritageplace.org, 10 A.M.–4 P.M. daily late May–mid-Oct.; last admission at 3 P.M.; adults $15.50, seniors $14, and kids 3–12 $10.50). Your first stop should be in the **museum** (open year-round; off-season: 10 A.M.–4 P.M. Mon.–Fri. mid-Oct.–late May), which traces the region's roots from the early First Nations people, through the first European contact, the fur trading and lumber eras, and the evolution of the Muskokas as a tourist destination.

More fun for the kids is the **pioneer village** (open seasonally), where wandering around the 20 restored buildings takes you back to the period between 1880 and 1910. Costumed interpreters demonstrate blacksmithing, woodworking, and other trades. You can also explore a trapper's cabin, a one-room schoolhouse, and a First Nations encampment.

You can also catch a ride on the *Portage*
Flyer steam train (100 Forbes Hill Dr., departs at noon, 1 P.M., 2 P.M., and 3 P.M., Tues.–Sat. July–Aug.; check website for off-season schedule; adults $5.25, seniors $4.75, and kids 3–12 $3.25), which ran from 1904 to 1959 in nearby Dwight, along the world's smallest commercial railroad. It operated on a 1.8-kilometer-long (1.125-mile) narrow-gauge track, as a "portage," ferrying supplies and tourists across a sliver of land between Peninsula Lake and Portage Bay.

The trip on the steam train today runs about 30 minutes and includes a stop at the **Rail Museum,** a re-creation of a 1920s train station, where you can learn more about the role of railroads and steamboats in the Muskokas' development. If you're a train enthusiast, note that the steam engine pulls the train only in July and August; in spring and fall, a diesel locomotive does the work, to help preserve the steam engine's life.

Muskoka Heritage Place is just a few minutes' drive from downtown Huntsville. From Main Street, just west of the bridge, go south on Brunel Road. The train depot is a short distance from the main entrance to Muskoka Heritage Place; watch for the signs.

Arrowhead Provincial Park

Through far smaller and less well known than nearby Algonquin, this provincial park (451 Arrowhead Park Rd., 705/789-5105, www.ontarioparks.com, $14/vehicle) is a worthwhile destination for day hiking, with several easy-to-moderate trails ranging from 1–7 kilometers (0.6–4.3 miles). In winter, these paths become cross-country ski trails (per day adults $9.50, kids 6–17 $4.75). Ski rentals are available, and you can also rent canoes, kayaks, and bicycles in the park. In July and August, go to the Beach Information Building at the day-use beach for rentals, and to the main park office in the spring and the fall.

The park is located 10 kilometers (six miles) north of Huntsville. If you're coming from Huntsville, take Highway 3 north; you can also reach the park via Highway 11.

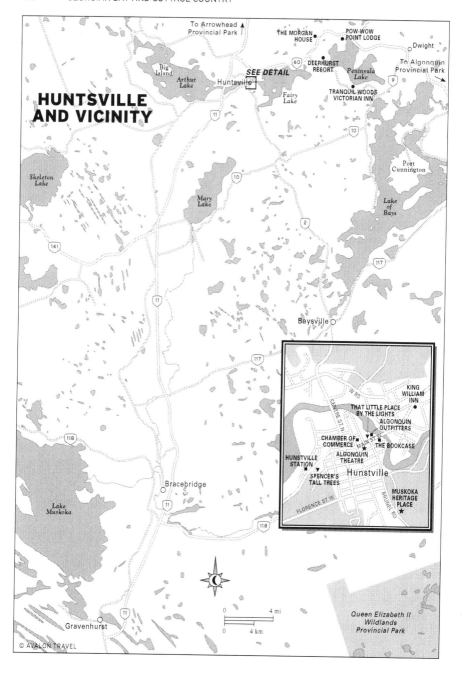

HUNTSVILLE AND VICINITY

To Arrowhead Provincial Park

THE MORGAN HOUSE

POW-WOW POINT LODGE

Dwight

SEE DETAIL

DEERHURST RESORT

Peninsula Lake

To Algonquin Provincial Park

Huntsville

Fairy Lake

TRANQUIL WOODS VICTORIAN INN

Big Island

Arthur Lake

Skeleton Lake

Mary Lake

Port Cunnington

Lake of Bays

Baysville

KING WILLIAM INN

THAT LITTLE PLACE BY THE LIGHTS

ALGONQUIN OUTFITTERS

CHAMBER OF COMMERCE

THE BOOKCASE

HUNSTVILLE STATION

ALGONQUIN THEATRE

Hunstville

SPENCER'S TALL TREES

MUSKOKA HERITAGE PLACE

FLORENCE ST W

BRUNEL RD

Bracebridge

Lake Muskoka

Gravenhurst

0   4 mi
0   4 km

Queen Elizabeth II Wildlands Provincial Park

© AVALON TRAVEL

Limberlost Forest and Wildlife Reserve

An excellent, less-visited hiking destination is the privately owned Limberlost Forest and Wildlife Reserve (South Limberlost Rd., 705/635-1584, www.limberlostlodges.com, dawn–dusk daily, free), where more than 70 kilometers (44 miles) of trails circle many of the property's 20 lakes as they crisscross the forested 4,045-hectare (10,000-acre) reserve. Check the website for the extremely detailed *Master Trail Guide,* which tells you about each of the trails and their notable features; it also includes trail maps. The trail guide is also available in the reserve office.

To find the reserve from Huntsville, follow Highway 60 east for about 10 kilometers (six miles), then turn left (north) onto Limberlost Road (Muskoka Road 8). Continue another nine kilometers (5.6 miles), and turn right onto South Limberlost Road and follow it for three kilometers (1.8 miles) to the reserve entrance. The gates of the reserve look rather imposing, but don't worry; pull up to the gates and they'll slide open.

ENTERTAINMENT AND SHOPPING

The **Algonquin Theatre** (37 Main St. E., 705/789-4975 or 888/696-4255, www.algonquintheatre.ca) stages concerts, plays, and lectures, featuring performers from near and far. All summer long, the **Huntsville Festival of the Arts** (705/789-4975, www.huntsvillefestival.on.ca) brings concerts, art workshops, and other events to venues around town. Many events are outdoors and free. For ticketed events, you can buy tickets online, by phone, or in person at the Algonquin Theatre.

What's a cottage holiday without time curled up with a good book? If you need something to read, stop into independent bookstore **The Bookcase** (93 Main St. E., 705/789-9111, www.thebookcase.ca, 10 A.M.–5 P.M. Mon.– Sat., noon–4 P.M. in spring; 9 A.M.–9 P.M. Mon.–Sat., 10 A.M.–5 P.M. Sun. in summer). Other shops along Huntsville's Main Street sell outdoor gear (useful if you need clothing or supplies for your excursions into Algonquin), artwork, and souvenirs. **Algonquin Outfitters Huntsville** (86 Main St. E., 705/787-0262 or 800/469-4948, www.algonquinoutfitters.com, 9:30 A.M.–6 P.M. Mon.–Wed., 9:30 A.M.–8 P.M. Thurs.–Fri., 9 A.M.–5:30 P.M. Sat., 11 A.M.–4 P.M. Sun. July–early Sept.; 10 A.M.–6 P.M. Mon.–Fri., 9 A.M.–5 P.M. Sat., 11 A.M.–4 P.M. Sun. early Sept.–June) has a large selection of outdoor clothing and gear. They also rent canoes, kayaks, and bikes.

ACCOMMODATIONS

The Huntsville area has a wide range of places to stay, from basic in-town motels, to B&Bs hidden in the woods, summer camp–style cottage colonies, and upscale resorts. A number of these accommodations are off Highway 60, just east of Huntsville. Closer to Algonquin's West Gate, in the tiny town of Dwight (which seems to exist primarily to provide lodging and other services to travelers heading into Algonquin), there's a cluster of accommodations around Oxtongue Lake.

Huntsville

The **King William Inn** (23 King William St., 705/789-9661 or 888/995-9169, www.kingwilliaminn.com, $129–165 d) is the nicest of the in-town motels. Although it sits on a charmless stretch of road opposite a fast-food joint and a car dealership, the King William has upgraded its rooms with crisp white linens and new furnishings. The standard rooms, with either two doubles or one double and one queen, are slightly smaller but otherwise similar to the queen rooms, which have one queen bed and a sleep sofa. The largest rooms are the kings with a whirlpool tub. Free Wi-Fi.

East of Huntsville

A stay at **The Morgan House** (83 Morgans Rd., 705/380-2566 or 866/311-1727, www.morganhousewoolworks.ca, $70 d, $100 d), a bed-and-breakfast in a comfortable, stone country home, is like a holiday with good friends on their (mostly) organic farm. Co-owner Pam Carnochan is a wool artist who also teaches at the Algonquin Art Centre, and she welcomes guests on the screened-in porch or in the parlor with its overstuffed furniture. Upstairs, the two simple guest rooms, with traditional quilts on the beds, share one large bathroom. Breakfast includes homemade baked goods and eggs from the farm's hens. Families are welcome.

A suburban home set amid lovely gardens, and, yes, tranquil woods, the **Tranquil Woods Victorian Inn** (50 North Portage Rd., 705/788-7235, www.tranquilwoods.ca, $120–135 d) is Victorian in style, but it's in a newly built house with high ceilings and an airy feel. Personable owners Judy and Dan enjoy helping guests organize their day and offer touring tips while serving up a hearty breakfast. The largest of the three guest rooms is on the main floor, with a private patio. Upstairs, the Red Oak room has a sleigh bed and Victorian furnishings, while the red-walled Scarlett Maple room is more country cottage.

Over breakfast at the █ **Pow-Wow Point Lodge** (207 Grassmere Resort Rd., 705/789-4951 or 800/461-4263, www.powwowpoint-lodge.com), staff ring a bell and announce the activities for the day, from sandcastle contests to swimming races to movie nights—just like at summer camp. And even if you don't go for organized fun, there's plenty to do, with a lakeside beach for swimming, canoeing, and kayaking, tennis courts, shuffleboard, a kids' play area, and an indoor pool for rainy days. Accommodations include basic, knotty pine–walled lodge rooms and cottages and more updated units, but all feel homey. Owners Doug and Dee Howell have been running the lodge since 1989, and many of their guests, including lots of multigenerational families, return year after year. Daily rates, which range $268–417 per person for a two-night stay, include three ample meals; kids' and teens' rates are discounted, and the daily rate is cheaper the longer you stay.

You won't be bored at the classy **Deerhurst Resort** (1235 Deerhurst Dr., 705/789-6411 or 800/461-4393, www.deerhurstresort.com, $239–719 d), where activities run the gamut from golf, tennis, squash, and Ping-Pong, to swimming, canoeing, kayaking, and more. The lakeside "Splash Zone" is summer fun central, with water trampolines, a climbing wall (anchored in the lake), beach volleyball, sunset

summer fun at the Deerhurst Resort

boat tours, and all kinds of watersports. The resort's sports desk organizes regular activities, too, including trail rides, kids' crafts, and both hiking and canoeing excursions to Algonquin Park. Accommodations at this sprawling property range from basic hotel rooms to condos with one, two, or three bedrooms (all the condos have full kitchens). You can spend a lot of time just navigating the grounds, so if you (and the kids) are going to spend most of your time at the lake, you might choose a room in the Bayshore building (it's right at the beach) or in one of the lakefront condos. If you'd rather be closer to the indoor pool, tennis courts, gym, spa, and restaurants, stay in the main inn or in one of the "sports villas." **Eclipse** is the resort's main dining room, serving contemporary fare overlooking the lake, but several more casual eateries are scattered around the property.

Dwight and Oxtongue Lake

If you don't want to camp, the cheapest beds in the Algonquin vicinity are at the laid-back **Wolf Den Bunkhouse and Cabins** (4568 Hwy. 60, Oxtongue Lake, 705/635-9336 or 866/271-9336, www.wolfdenbunkhouse.com, year-round, $25 dorm, $42 s, $66–84 d, $80–135 cabins), a hostel located between Dwight and the park's West Gate. It's not as picturesque as lakeside lodgings, but it's a friendly spot, where you can often meet other travelers to explore Algonquin Park. The main lodge has a shared kitchen and large lounge, as well as several guest rooms (each accommodating one or two people) on the lower level. Two log bunkhouses each have an eight-bed dorm on the upper floor and rooms sleeping four to five on the main level. Two more private cabins with kitchenettes sleep four to six. In addition to a shared washroom in the main lodge, there's a wash house with showers, toilets, and sinks in the center of the property, but none of the units has a private bath. There's no meal service, so bring your own provisions.

A small cluster of lodgings sits along Oxtongue Lake, just off Highway 60, about a 10-minute drive from Algonquin's West Gate. It's a pretty setting, although the proximity

of Highway 60 and its traffic noise can be bothersome.

Under the same ownership as the Bartlett Lodge in Algonquin Park, **The Pines Cottage Resort** (1032 Oxtongue Lake Rd., Dwight, 705/635-2379, www.algonquinparkaccommodations.com, late May–mid-Oct., $125–225) has several family-friendly one- and two-bedroom cottages (with fully equipped kitchens) in the woods just above Oxtongue Lake, where there's a sandy beach. Rates include the use of canoes and kayaks.

More modern, but a little closer to Highway 60, the **Blue Spruce Resort** (4308 Hwy. 60, Dwight, 705/635-2330, www.bluespruce.ca, $132–303) has both hotel-style suites and standalone cottages, ranging from one to three bedrooms, all with kitchens. There are tennis courts and a swimming beach, with a water trampoline. The Blue Spruce, which has Wi-Fi as well as a coin-operated laundry for guests, is open year-round.

Camping

Arrowhead Provincial Park (451 Arrowhead Park Rd., 705/789-5105, www.ontarioparks.com, $14/vehicle) has three campgrounds (mid-May–mid-Oct., $32.52 tent sites, $37.39 electric sites), with a total of 378 campsites, 185 with electrical service. The campgrounds have comfort stations with flush toilets and showers.

FOOD
Huntsville

Two of the best spots for picnic supplies or a meal to go are located on Highway 60, just east of town, and both have similar names. The **Farmer's Daughter** (118 Hwy. 60, 705/789.5700, www.fresheverything.ca, 8 a.m.–6 p.m. Mon.–Wed., 8 a.m.–7 p.m. Thurs.–Fri., 9 a.m.–6 p.m. Sat., 9 a.m.–5 p.m. Sun.) is a combination farm stand, prepared food counter, bakery, and gourmet market. They sell fresh produce, sandwiches made to order, and fancy fixings like smoked fish pâté or homemade jams. Their baked goods, including the addictive trail mix bars, are excellent. If your accommodations have a kitchen, you can pick up dishes like macaroni and cheese or chicken pot pie to heat up back at the cottage.

Across the road, the **Butcher's Daughters** (133 Hwy. 60, 705/789-2848, www.butchersdaughters.ca, 9 A.M.–6 P.M. Mon.–Sat., 10 A.M.–4 P.M. Sun. July–Aug.; 9 A.M.–6 P.M. Mon.–Sat. June and Sept., 9 A.M.–6 P.M. Tues.–Sat. Oct.–May, $4.50–8) makes good deli sandwiches, including the popular peameal bacon, as well as interesting soups and salads. There's a small seating area, or you can take your food to go. They also make heat-and-eat main dishes like lasagna, shepherd's pie, or beef bourguignon, useful if you have kitchen facilities.

For many Ontarians, a trip to Cottage Country isn't complete without a stop at the old-style, family-friendly **West Side Fish and Chips** (126 Main St. W., 705/789-7200, 8 A.M.–8 P.M. daily, $4–15) for a hearty plate of halibut and chips and a gooey slice of coconut cream pie. They're always busy, but you can amuse yourself with trivia game cards while you wait.

You know **That Little Place by the Lights** (76 Main St. E., 705/789-2536, www.thatlittleplacebythelights.ca, 9 A.M.–9 P.M. Mon.–Sat., 11 A.M.–4 P.M. Sun., lunch $5–10, dinner $11–14)? It's a cozy Italian trattoria masquerading as a touristy ice cream parlor and coffee shop. The sauces for the pastas and pizzas are homemade (try the spicy, salty linguini puttanesca, with olives, capers, anchovies, and hot peppers), and the salads are simple but fresh. It's family friendly, too, especially if you promise the kids some gelato for dessert.

One of Huntsville's highly regarded upscale restaurants is **Spencer's Tall Trees** (87 Main St. W., 705/789-9769, www.spencerstalltrees.com, 5 P.M.–close Mon., 11:30 A.M.–2 P.M. and 5 P.M.–close Tues.–Fri., 5 P.M.–close Sat., call for seasonal hours, lunch $10–21, dinner $18–49) set in a heritage house amid the trees. They serve updated versions of classics like filet mignon with béarnaise sauce, veal Oscar (topped with crab), or pickerel in a maple-thyme-butter sauce. Lunch options range from lighter salads and sandwiches to pastas. To finish with

something sweet, try the chocolate pâté or a seasonal fruit crumble.

Dwight and Oxtongue Lake

The perpetual lines attest to the popularity of **Henrietta's Pine Bakery** (2868 Hwy. 60, Dwight, 705/635-2214, 9 A.M.–5 P.M. daily May–mid-Oct.), where the specialties include sticky buns and a highly-recommended scone-like cranberry pastry called the Muskoka cloud. They do sell breads and other savories, but it's the sweets that make it worth the stop. Come early in the day, since they close early if they sell out of goodies.

INFORMATION AND SERVICES

The **Huntsville/Lake of Bays Chamber of Commerce** (8 West St. N., 705/789-4771, www.huntsvilleadventures.com), just off Main Street, can provide more information about events and things to do in the Huntsville/Algonquin region.

Algonquin Outfitters Oxtongue Lake (1035 Algonquin Outfitters Rd., Dwight, 705/635-2243 or 800/469-4948, www.algonquinoutfitters.com, 8 A.M.–6 P.M. Mon.–Thurs., 8 A.M.–7 P.M. Fri.–Sun. July–early Sept.; 9 A.M.–5 P.M. Mon.–Thurs., 8 A.M.–6 P.M. Fri.–Sat., 9 A.M.–6 P.M. Sun. May–June and early Sept.–mid-Oct.; 9 A.M.–5 P.M. daily mid-Oct.–Apr.) stocks outdoor clothing and gear; rents canoes, kayaks, and bikes; and offers guided canoe and kayak trips in and around Algonquin Park.

GETTING THERE
By Car

Huntsville is 215 kilometers (133 miles) north of Toronto and 35 kilometers (22 miles) north of Bracebridge. From Toronto, pick up Highway 400 north to Barrie, then continue north on Highway 11 to Huntsville.

By Train

Ontario Northland (800/461-8558, www.ontarionorthland.ca, 3 hours, one-way adults $48.15, seniors and students, $40.90, kids 2–11 $24.10) runs the convenient *Northlander* train from Toronto's Union Station to **Huntsville Station** (26 Station Rd.), just off Main Street west of downtown. From Huntsville, trains continue to North Bay, Temagami, Cochrane, and other points north. The *Northlander* operates Sunday through Friday.

By Bus

Ontario Northland (705/789-6431 or 800/461-8558, www.ontarionorthland.ca, 3.75–4 hours, one-way adults $48.15, seniors and students, $40.90, kids 2–11 $24.10) operates buses to Huntsville from the Toronto Central Bus Station on Bay Street. The bus is a little slower than the train (the fares are the same), but departures are more frequent. The **Huntsville Bus Depot** (77 Centre St. N.) is one kilometer (0.6 mile) north of Main Street. Buses continue from Huntsville to North Bay, Temagami, Cochrane, and other northern destinations.

If you're coming to Huntsville directly from Toronto's Pearson airport, you can take the **Shuttle Ontario** (317 Carmichael Dr., North Bay, 705/474-7942 or 800/461-4219, www.shuttleontario.com, 2.75 hours, one-way adults $91) shared van service, which runs two scheduled trips a day in each direction. It's convenient, since it takes you right from the airport, but it's much more expensive than the Ontario Northland trains or buses.

GETTING AROUND

While it's easy to get to Huntsville without a car, and the downtown area is quite compact, exploring the region around the town, including Algonquin Park, is difficult without your own wheels. If you don't have your own car, take the bus or train into Huntsville and then rent a car for a couple of days to explore Algonquin. **Enterprise Rent-A-Car** (174 Main St. W., 705/789-1834 or 800/736-8222, www.enterpriserentacar.ca) has an office on the west end of Main Street. **Discount Car Rentals** (10 Howland Dr., 705/788-3737, www.discountcar.com) is north of town.

Algonquin Provincial Park

If you visit only one of Ontario's many outdoor destination, the province's first provincial park is an excellent choice. Measuring 763,000 hectares (1,885,000 acres), Algonquin Provincial Park (www.ontarioparks.com or www.algonquinpark.on.ca) is not just big—it's massive, stretching across a wide swath of Northeastern Ontario. Covered with hardwood and coniferous forests, the region was a major logging area in the 1800s, and many visitors are surprised to learn that limited logging is still allowed in some sections of the park. When the park was created in 1893, it wasn't to bring a halt to logging, but rather to protect the region's wildlife.

The park's earliest tourists arrived by train, disembarking at a rail depot near Cache Lake in the southwest quadrant of the park; a nearby hotel housed passengers from Toronto and points south. In the 1930s, Highway 60 was built across Algonquin's southern sections. Sadly, as more and more tourists came by road, the rail service was discontinued. The prevailing wisdom at the time was that eliminating train service would keep the park more "natural."

Highway 60 is still the main access route for most park visitors entering the West Gate from Huntsville (or Toronto) or the East Gate from Ottawa. If your time is limited, pick a few stops—perhaps a paddle at Canoe Lake, hiking one or two of the shorter trails—and spend an hour at the exhibits in the park Visitor Centre.

Despite the park's popularity, you can still find plenty of quiet trails and canoe routes to explore even if you stay near Highway 60. But Algonquin also has a vast backcountry, offering ample opportunities to get out into the wilderness. Most of Algonquin's backcountry is reachable only by canoe.

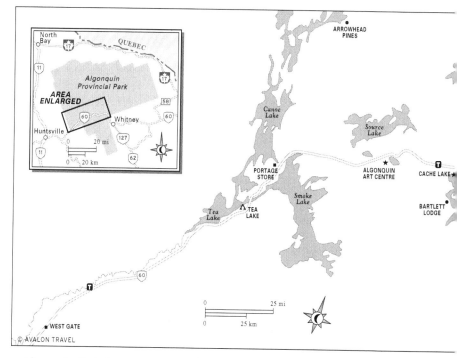

Algonquin Park is open year-round, although many park services and sights operate only from April or May until mid-October.

SIGHTS

The park's main sights are listed from west to east along Highway 60, the direction you'll reach them if coming from Toronto or from elsewhere in the Muskoka region. Distances are from the park's West Gate, so a sight at "KM 20" is 20 kilometers east of the West Gate. If coming from Ottawa, Peterborough, and the Kawarthas, or from elsewhere in Eastern Ontario, enter the park from the East Gate (at KM 56) and follow these locations in reverse.

West Gate (Hwy. 60, KM 0)

At Algonquin's western entrance, you can purchase your park permit ($16.25/vehicle), which all visitors must have. (If you're simply driving across the park on Highway 60 without

stopping, you do not need a park permit. If you stop anywhere in the park, even to use the bathroom, you need to have a permit, or you risk being fined.) Display the permit on your dashboard, so that it's visible from outside. If the park warden can't see the permit, you'll get a ticket. Permits are available at the East and West Gates and at the Algonquin Park Visitor Centre.

If you're going to spend several days in the park, or if you're visiting multiple parks, consider purchasing an **Ontario Parks seasonal pass,** which allows unlimited day visits to any Ontario provincial parks. You can buy a summer-only pass (valid Apr.–Nov., $107.50), a winter-only pass (Dec.–Mar., $70), or a full-year pass valid from April until the following March ($150.50)

The on-site staff can help you get oriented and provide information about things to see and do, which is particularly helpful if your time is limited.

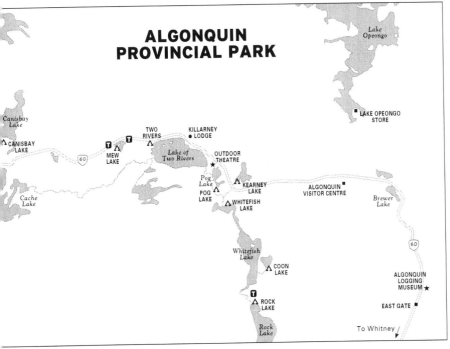

Canoe Lake (Hwy. 60, KM 14.1)

The history of Canoe Lake is inextricably linked to the mysterious disappearance of the painter Tom Thomson (1877–1917), a member of the Group of Seven artists who lived and worked in Ontario in the early 1900s. Thomson spent several years visiting and painting in Algonquin Park, beginning in 1912, mostly on and around Canoe Lake. Thomson was last seen on July 8, 1917, in the vicinity of Canoe Lake—and then he vanished. His overturned canoe was found behind the lake's Wapomeo Island, and several days later, his body was pulled from the lake. The exact circumstances of his death remain a puzzle that has never been solved. In his memory, the **Tom Thomson memorial cairn** was erected in 1930 on one of Thomson's favorite Canoe Lake campsites. The cairn is accessible only by canoe.

The **Portage Store** (Hwy. 60, KM 14.1, 705/633-5622, www.portagestore.com, late Apr.–mid-Oct.) on Canoe Lake rents canoes

and can give you tips on where to go, including how to get to the Thomson cairn. They also offer half- and full-day guided paddles.

Algonquin Art Centre (Hwy. 60, KM 20)

This art center (705/633-5555, www.algonquinartcentre.com, 10 A.M.–5 P.M. daily June–mid-Oct.) has a small gallery (admission by donation) that shows changing exhibits of works by artists who have an Algonquin connection. The center also offers drop-in art activities (10:30 A.M.–4:30 P.M. daily July–Aug.), for both children and adults, which are great for a rainy day or when the kids need a break from hiking and swimming. You might paint a wooden canoe paddle or miniature canoe, make a mobile, or create a clay sculpture. Activities take place in a screened outdoor gazebo. Prices vary by activity, but most range $10–25. On Tuesdays, Wednesdays, and Thursdays in summer, the

HOWLING WITH THE WOLVES

One of the many animals who live in the Algonquin Provincial Park wilderness is the wolf. And one of the most popular (and eeriest) activities at Algonquin Park is the Wolf Howl.

These events typically attract more than 1,500 visitors, who assemble at the park's Outdoor Theatre (Hwy. 60, KM 35.4) for a presentation about wolves and their habitat. Then everyone gets in their cars and drives caravan-style to a designated spot where park naturalists have heard a wolf pack on the previous night. Once everyone is in place, the naturalists begin a sequence of howls – hoping that the wolves will respond with howls of their own. Sometimes they do, and sometimes they don't, but if you're lucky enough to hear the wolf pack howling, it's a unique experience.

The Wolf Howls are typically held during the month of August (or occasionally the first week of September), the only time of year when wolves are likely to remain in one place for days at a time. The howls are held once a week, on Thursday evenings, beginning at 8 P.M., and last about three hours.

Check event bulletin boards throughout the park, or phone the Visitor Centre (613/637-2828) to confirm if the week's Wolf Howl will be held. Howls are canceled if no wolves are in an area (along Hwy. 60) or if the weather is inclement, so you generally won't know till the day of the event whether it will take place. Updates on the Wolf Howls are also posted on the Friends of Algonquin Park website (www.algonquinpark.on.ca), where you can sign up to receive an email update on the week's Wolf Howl.

---

art center runs art classes, as well, for children and adults. Suitable for beginning and more advanced students, the classes typically last 90 minutes. Pre-registration is required; call or visit the center in advance to sign up.

Cache Lake (Hwy. 60, KM 23.5)

Cache Lake was once the center of activity in Algonquin Park. From the 1890s, when the park was first established, until the 1950s, this lake area had a rail depot—Algonquin Park Station—as well as a large hotel. All that remains today, aside from the lovely lake itself, is a short historical walking trail, where several signs with historical photos along a wooded path tell you about the area's interesting past.

Another reason to stop at Cache Lake is to eat or stay at **Bartlett Lodge** (Cache Lake, 705/633-5543, 705/633-5746, or 866/614-5355, www.bartlettlodge.com, mid-May–late Oct.). Boat service to the lodge runs across the lake from the Cache Lake Landing.

Lake of Two Rivers (Hwy. 60, KM 31)

Lake of Two Rivers is a busy place. In addition to the large **Two Rivers Campground** (519/826-5290 or 888/668-7275, www.ontarioparks.com, reservation fee $9.50 phone, $8.50 online, $35.25–40.50 tent sites, $46 RV sites), there's a snack bar, grocery store, and mountain bike rentals. East of the campground, **Killarney Lodge** (Lake of Two Rivers, Hwy. 60, KM 33.2, 705/633-5551 or 866/473-5551, www.killarney-lodge.com) is set on the Lake of Two Rivers. Just east of the lodge is a public swimming beach.

Algonquin Visitor Centre (Hwy. 60, KM 43)

Even if you've entered the park from the west and gotten oriented at the West Gate, it's worth stopping into the Algonquin Visitor Centre (9 A.M.–5 P.M. daily late Apr.–late June and mid–late Oct.; 9 A.M.–9 P.M. daily late June–early Sept.; 9 A.M.–6 P.M. daily early Sept.–mid-Oct.; 10 A.M.–4 P.M. Sat.–Sun. Nov.–late Apr., with daily hours during holiday weeks) to learn more about the park. Start by watching a 12-minute film about the park's history and natural features, and then visit the exhibit area, which covers these topics in more detail. In summer, many of the park's interpretive programs are based at the Visitor Centre. A shop sells detailed park maps and guides, as well as books about wildlife, camping, and the outdoors. There's a basic cafeteria, and free Wi-Fi, too. The best feature of the Visitor Centre, though, is outside the building. The deck out back overlooks a wide swath of park territory and helps you appreciate Algonquin's vast expanse.

Algonquin Logging Museum (Hwy. 60, KM 54.5)

Logging was an important part of Algonquin's heritage, and you can learn more about that history and about the delicate balance between industry and preservation at the Algonquin Logging Museum (9 A.M.–5 P.M. daily late June–mid-Oct., free). Inside the exhibit building, you can watch a short video about Algonquin's logging history, but the most interesting parts of this museum are outdoors. Follow a walking trail through a re-created logging camp, continuing along the trail, where you can see how loggers cut and squared the trees, hauled them across the lakes, and drove them through water "chutes" to transport them down the river to the cities. You can climb aboard an "alligator," a steam-powered tugboat used to haul logs. The trail also takes you past a working log dam and chute, a restored blacksmith shop, a locomotive, and a classic 1950s truck. There are enough things to touch and climb on that kids may enjoy it, even if they don't appreciate the historical angle.

East Gate (Hwy. 60, KM 55.8)

Like the West Gate, Algonquin's eastern entrance has an information office that sells the required park permits ($16.25/vehicle), provides park maps, and offers suggestions about things to see and do. There's no need to stop here if you're coming from the west and leaving the park, although if you're driving east toward Ottawa, you might stop and use the restrooms before hitting the road.

SPORTS AND RECREATION
Bicycling

Algonquin Park has two cycling trails that are easy to reach from Highway 60. The 10-kilometer (6.2-mile) **Old Railway Bike Trail** follows the route of a former rail line. Connecting the Mew Lake and Rock Lake Campgrounds, the trail also passes the campgrounds at Lake of Two Rivers, Kearney Lake, Pog Lake, Whitefish Lake, and Coon Lake. The trail is relatively flat and good for families.

The **Minnesing Mountain Bike Trail** (Hwy. 60, KM 23, mid-June–mid-Oct.) is more challenging; the park rates it as "moderate" on the scale of technical difficulty. It includes four hilly loops of 4.7, 10.1, 17.1, and 23.4 kilometers (2.9, 6.3, 10.6, and 14.5 miles). The trail is often quite muddy in June and July.

You can rent bikes at the **Two Rivers Store** (Hwy. 60, KM 31.4, 705/633-5622) and the **Opeongo Store** (Lake Opeongo, 6.2 kilometers, or 3.9 miles, north of KM 46.3, 613/637-2075 or 888/280-8886, www.algonquinoutfitters.com).

Canoeing

Algonquin Park (www.ontarioparks.com or www.algonquinpark.on.ca) is one of Ontario's most popular destinations for canoeing. Not only can you paddle on the park's numerous lakes and rivers, but Algonquin also has more than 2,000 kilometers (1,240 miles) of canoe routes across the backcountry, ideal for overnight or multiday canoe trips. A useful planning resource is the *Canoe Routes of Algonquin Provincial Park Map* (www.algonquinpark.on.ca, $4.95), which you can order online or purchase at any of the park stores or information centers. It details all the lakes, access points, portages, and campsites across Algonquin.

Within the park, you can rent canoes at the **Portage Store** (Canoe Lake, Hwy. 60, KM 14.1) and the Opeongo Store (6.2 km or 3.9 miles north of KM 46.3), run by **Algonquin Outfitters** (613/637-2075 or 888/280-8886, www.algonquinoutfitters.com). Both outfitters offer shuttle services to take you and your canoe to various launch points. Many outfitters outside the park will rent canoes with car-top carriers, so you can transport them to launch points in Algonquin.

If you're new to canoeing, or if you'd prefer to go out with a guide, both the Portage Store and Algonquin Outfitters offer guided canoe day trips. The Portage Store runs a full-day trip (9:30 A.M.–4:30 P.M., adults $57.95, kids under 14 $29) on Canoe Lake, which includes an orientation about the park, basic canoe instruction, and a daylong paddle with a stop for a picnic lunch. Trips run daily from late June through early September, and every day except Tuesday and Thursday from mid-May to late June and from early September to mid-October. In July and August, they also offer a half-day trip (1–5 P.M., adults $32.95, kids under 14 $17. Reservations are recommended for both trips.

Algonquin Outfitters' guided day trips include departures from the Opeongo Store and from their location just outside the park's West Gate on Oxtongue Lake. From the Opeongo Store, options include a half-day Costello Creek trip (Mon.–Fri. mid-May–Oct., $69.98/person for two, $46.98/person for three, $34.98/person for four) and a full-day Hailstorm Creek nature-reserve trip (Mon.–Fri. mid-May–Oct., $152.48/person for two, $121.65/person for three, $111.23/person for four). They also offer a full-day guided canoe trip (Mon.–Fri. mid-May–Oct., $139.98/person for two, $93.98/person for three, $69.98/person for four) departing from their Oxtongue Lake store at 9 A.M. Rates for kids are discounted by 25 percent.

Hiking

All along the Highway 60 corridor are trails for day hikes, ranging from an easy boardwalk path to strenuous all-day excursions. More experienced hikers can tromp along more than 140 kilometers (87 miles) of backpacking trails through the park's interior.

Following are the most accessible park trails, their locations along Highway 60, their length, and difficulty:

• Whiskey Rapids (KM 7.2, 2.1 km, moderate)
• Hardwood Lookout (KM 13.8, 0.8 km, moderate)
• Mizzy Lake (KM 15.4, 11 km, moderate)
• Peck Lake (KM 19.2, 1.9 km, moderate)
• Track and Tower (KM 25, 7.7 km, moderate)
• Hemlock Bluff (KM 27.2, 3.5 km, moderate)
• Bat Lake (KM 30, 5.6 km, moderate)
• Two Rivers (KM 31, 2.1 km, moderate)
• Centennial Ridges (KM 37.6, 10 km, strenuous)
• Lookout (KM 39.7, 1.9 km, moderate)
• Big Pines (KM 40.3, 2.9 km, moderate)
• Booth's Rock (KM 40.5, 5.1 km, moderate)
• Spruce Bog Boardwalk (KM 42.5, 1.5 km, easy)
• Beaver Pond (KM 45.2, 2 km, moderate)

Trail guides, with more details about each of these hikes, are available at the trailheads (from spring through fall) and online (www.algonquinpark.on.ca).

Winter Sports

If you want to try dogsledding, these outfitters can get you out on the Algonquin trails. **Voyageur Quest** (416/486-3605 or 800/794-9660, www.voyageurquest.com) offers an introductory day of dogsledding (Dec.–Mar., $185/person) that includes orientation, harnessing the dogs, and a four-hour mush. They also offer weekend-long and multiday dogsledding trips.

Snow Forest Adventures (705/783-0461, www.snowforestadventures.ca) runs half-day (10 A.M.–12:30 P.M. or 1–3:30 P.M., late Dec.–Mar., $125/person) and full-day (10 A.M.–3 P.M. late Dec.–Mar., $190/person) dogsledding trips that depart from the Sunday Lake dogsledding trails (Hwy. 60, KM 40). No experience is necessary, and kids under 12 can ride on a sled with a paying adult for a small fee ($25/half-day trip, $50/full-day trip).

Algonquin Provincial Park is a popular destination for hikers.

Algonquin Park has three areas that offer trails for cross-country skiing. At the West Gate, the groomed **Fen Lake Ski Trail** has four loops, ranging 1.25–13 kilometers (0.75–8 miles). One kilometer (0.6 mile) west of the East Gate, the groomed **Leaf Lake Trail** has routes measuring 5–51 kilometers (3–32 miles). For more challenging wilderness skiing, head to the **Minnesing Trail** (Hwy. 60, KM 23), where four ungroomed loops range 4.7–23.4 kilometers (2.9–14.5 miles).

For snowshoeing, you can explore nearly anywhere in the park, including any of the hiking trails along the Highway 60 corridor. Snowshoes are not allowed on the cross-country trails.

You must have a park permit ($16.25/vehicle) for any winter activities. Also remember that daylight is much more limited in the winter, so make sure you have ample time to get off the trails before dark. Ensure, too, that you have warm clothes, particularly hats, gloves, boots, and multiple layers appropriate for your outdoor activity.

Outfitters

A number of outfitters, both within and outside Algonquin Park, can help you organize canoeing, camping, and hiking trips; rent you the gear you need; or take you on a guided journey. Some even organize dogsledding excursions.

Algonquin Outfitters (800/469-4948, www.algonquinoutfitters.com) has locations throughout the Muskoka region, including the Opeongo Store on Lake Opeongo within the park, Oxtongue Lake outside the West Gate, and Huntsville. They offer a variety of services and trips, including half-day, full-day, and multiday canoe and kayak trips, either guided or self-guided, departing from several different locations.

Located on Canoe Lake, the **Portage Store** (Hwy. 60, KM 14.1, 705/633-5622, www.portagestore.com, late Apr.–mid-Oct.) organizes canoe trips and offers half-, full-, and multiday guided paddles.

Outside the East Gate, **Opeongo Outfitters** (Hwy. 60, Whitney, 613/637-5470 or 800/790-1864, www.opeongooutfitters.com, mid-Apr.–mid-Oct.) can rent the gear you need for a multiday canoe trip, including a canoe, tent, a pack, a sleeping bag, food, cooking utensils, and other supplies. You can also rent a kayak or canoe for the day.

Voyageur Quest (416/486-3605 or 800/794-9660, www.voyageurquest.com) organizes several different Algonquin excursions, from three- to five-day canoe trips (including trips designed for families), to winter dogsledding trips.

Snow Forest Adventures (705/783-0461, www.snowforestadventures.ca) offers half-day and full-day dogsledding trips, from late December through March, weather permitting.

ACCOMMODATIONS AND FOOD

If you want to stay within the park, you can choose from three upscale lodges (which also operate restaurants), rustic former ranger cabins, or camping. The lodges, cabins, and most of the campgrounds are open from spring to fall. In winter, you can camp at Mew Lake, off Highway 60, or out in the backcountry. The park cafeterias and snack bars also operate seasonally.

Park Lodges

From hiking to swimming to canoeing, there's plenty to do at **Arowhon Pines** (Arowhon Rd., 705/633-5661 or 866/633-5661, www.arowhonpines.ca, late May–mid-Oct., $198–440/person). When you're ready to bed down for the night, you can choose from 50 rooms, in either shared or private cabins. The private cabins are just that: your own cottage, with a queen bed, lounge area, and private deck. The shared cabins come in two flavors. In the two-bedroom cabins, you have a private room and bath, but share the lounge space with guests in the other room. The shared cabins are more like mini-lodges, where your room and bath are private, but all the guests use the common living area. Lodging rates, which include breakfast, lunch, and dinner, as well as use of all the recreational facilities, go up depending on the level of privacy. To reach Arowhon Pines, follow Highway 60 to KM16, then turn north onto Arowhon Rd., which winds through the woods to the lodge.

Getting to **Bartlett Lodge** (Cache Lake, 705/633-5543, 705/633-5746, or 866/614-5355, www.bartlettlodge.com, mid-May–late Oct.) is half the fun. Set on the opposite side of Cache Lake from Highway 60, the lodge is accessible only by boat. They run a motorboat shuttle to bring guests back and forth, making a stay here feel like a true getaway into the woods. Most of the accommodations are in cottages, ranging from studios to three bedrooms. The studio units ($155–185/person), in a historic log cabin, are named for Group of Seven artists A. Y. Jackson and Lawren Harris and feature the artists' work. Some of the cabins ($167–238/person) were built back in the early 1900s, while others were constructed more recently; they're all lakeside or a short walk away. Rates in the studios and cabins include a buffet breakfast and a multicourse dinner. The lodge also offers a "glamping" (glamorous camping) option: accommodations in two furnished **platform tents** ($80–100/person), which are more like staying in an outdoor room than camping in a tent. A washroom with showers is in an adjacent building. Tent rates include a buffet breakfast. To get to Bartlett Lodge, turn off Highway 60 at KM 23.5, Cache Lake. Park your car and use the lodge phone at Cache Lake Landing to contact the lodge. They'll send their water taxi to pick you up.

Killarney Lodge (Lake of Two Rivers, Hwy. 60, KM 33.2, 705/633-5551 or 866/473-5551, www.killarneylodge.com, mid-May–mid-Oct., $169–339/person) is the easiest to reach of the park lodges. Just off Highway 60, it's a convenient base for exploring the rest of the park. The 25 log cottages are set in the woods, with neat-as-a-pin knotty-pine or rough-hewn log interiors. The "one-bedroom" cabins are one room, with a king or queen bed; the "two-bedroom" cabins have two rooms, one with a king bed, a second with twin beds. Most (but not all) of the cottages are right on the lake, and each comes with your own canoe.

Ranger Cabins

Algonquin has 14 ranger cabins (mid-Apr.–mid-Oct., $58–134) that essentially offer indoor camping. They're rustic log structures without running water or electricity that were built in the early 1900s; rangers patrolling the park would travel from cabin to cabin where they'd overnight. You can reach five of the cabins by car, including cabins at Rain Lake, Bissett Creek Road, Kiosk, and two cabins at Brent. The remainder are in the backcountry. The cabins are basic, equipped with a table and chairs, a wood stove, and an outdoor toilet; most have bunks but not necessarily mattresses, so bring a sleeping pad as well as a sleeping bag. You also need to bring any dishes, pots, or cooking utensils that you want.

The Friends of Algonquin Park (www.algonquinpark.on.ca) has detailed descriptions of each cabin and their facilities.

Camping

Algonquin is a popular destination for campers, with the largest number of campsites of any Ontario provincial park. Reserve your campsite (519/826-5290 or 888/668-7275, www.ontarioparks.com, reservation fee $9.50 phone, $8.50 online, $35.25–40.50 tent sites, $46 RV sites) in advance, particularly for summer and fall weekends. Eight of the front-country campgrounds are accessible by car near Highway 60. Most are seasonal, opening in late April or mid-May and closing in mid-October. Only the Mew Lake campground is open year-round.

The front-country campgrounds (and their distance from the West Gate) are:

- Tea Lake (KM 11.4, 42 sites) has pit toilets and no other facilities.
- Canisbay Lake (KM 23.1, 242 sites) has secluded campsites, swimming beaches, showers, and flush toilets.
- Mew Lake (KM 30.6, 131 sites) also has seven **yurts** ($91.50/night), available year-round. The yurts, which sleep six, are furnished with two sets of bunk beds (a double below and a single above), a table and chairs, a propane barbecue, cooking utensils, and dishes. They

have electric lights and heat. You still need to bring sleeping bags or other bedding, as well as food and other personal items.

- Two Rivers (KM 31.8, 241 sites) is the most centrally located, and frequently the most crowded. It has a beach, a laundry, flush toilets, and showers.
- Pog Lake (KM 36.9, 286 sites) has secluded campsites, and comfort stations with showers, laundry, and flush toilets.
- Kearney Lake (KM 36.5, 103 sites) has two beaches, showers, and flush toilets.
- Coon Lake (six kilometers south of KM 40.3, 48 sites) has a beach and pit toilets.
- Rock Lake (eight kilometers south of KM 40.3, 121 sites) has two beaches, showers, flush toilets, and laundry.

Algonquin has three more drive-in campgrounds (late Apr.–mid-Oct.) farther north. **Achray** (45 sites), **Brent** (30 sites), and **Kiosk** (22 sites) campgrounds are all accessible from Highway 17 but far more secluded than the Highway 60 camping areas. Achray and Kiosk have flush toilets, and Achray also has a yurt, but none of these three campgrounds has showers.

Algonquin Park also has numerous **backcountry campgrounds** (adults $11.75, kids 6–17 $5) that you can't reach by car; most are accessible only by canoe. The Friends of Algonquin Park (www.algonquinpark.on.ca) has detailed information to help plan a trip into the backcountry. Several outfitters also organize backcountry trips.

Outside the Park

A short drive outside the park's East Gate, the **Couples Resort** (Galeairy Lake Rd., Whitney, 866/202-1179, www.couplesresort.ca, $152–798 d) has an entirely different ambience than the cottage-style park lodges. The decor, in the 36 suites and 12 cabins, all within 15 meters (50 feet) of the waterfront, is unabashedly romantic, even over-the-top, designed for couples who want to cocoon. Many rooms, which range from large to huge, have four-poster beds, ornate wallpapers and window treatments, hot tubs or whirlpool baths (or both), as well as wood-burning fireplaces and iPod docks with CD players and radios. If you ever come out of your room, you can have a dip in the outdoor heated saltwater pool (late May–mid-Oct.), play pool or table tennis, take a sauna, or work out in the fitness room. There's an on-site spa, too.

Prices include breakfast, served either in the dining room or in your suite, and a five-course dinner. Plan to dress for dinner; jeans, shorts, and sandals are forbidden, and men must wear a dress shirt with a collar. If you must get online, Internet access is available ($20/stay). Check the resort website for midweek or last-minute specials.

Couples Resort is in the town of Whitney. From Highway 60, go south on Galeairy Lake Road.

Food

If you're not a lodge guest, you can still come for a meal in the dining room at **Arowhon Pines** (Arowhon Rd., 705/633-5661 or 866/633-5661, www.arowhonpines.ca, late May–mid-Oct.). Meals are a fixed price: breakfast (8–10 A.M., $25/person), weekday lunch (12:30–2 P.M., $32/person), weekend lunch buffet (12:30–2 P.M., $45/person), and an abundant multicourse dinner (6:30 P.M. only, $70/person). The dining room doesn't have a license to serve alcohol, but you can bring your own.

The **Bartlett Lodge** dining room (Cache Lake, 705/633-5543, 705/633-5746, or 866/614-5355, www.bartlettlodge.com, mid-May–late Oct.) is open to nonguests for breakfast ($15/person) and in the evening, when an elaborate five-course, prix-fixe dinner ($59/person) is served; kids have a three-course dinner option ($25/person). The dining room isn't licensed to serve alcohol, but you can bring your own.

The main lodge building at **Killarney Lodge** (Lake of Two Rivers, Hwy. 60, KM 33.2, 705/633-5551 or 866/473-5551, www.killarney-lodge.com, mid-May–mid-Oct.) dates to 1935 and now houses the dining room. The dining room is open to the public, serving hearty, fixed-price, three-course menus at lunch (noon–2 P.M. daily, $25) and dinner (5:45 P.M.–7:30 P.M., $50). If you're not a lodge guest, reservations

are recommended for dinner. Also, the dining room keeps slightly shorter hours in May and June, so phone to confirm.

In addition to the lodges' dining rooms, you can get casual meals at the **Portage Store** (Canoe Lake, Hwy. 60, KM 14.1, 705/633-5622, www.portagestore.com), which serves breakfast, lunch, and dinner from late April through mid-October, and at the **Sunday Creek Café** (Hwy. 60, KM 63, 613/637-1133), the basic cafeteria in the Algonquin Visitor Centre. A seasonal snack bar sells sandwiches and ice cream at the **Two Rivers Store** (Hwy. 60, KM 31.4).

INFORMATION AND SERVICES

For general information about Algonquin Park, phone the **Algonquin Park Information Office** (705/633-5572, 9 A.M.–4 P.M. daily Apr.–Oct., 9 A.M.–4 P.M. Fri.–Sun. Nov.–Mar., www.algonquinpark.on.ca). You can also get visitor information at the park's West Gate, East Gate, and Visitor Centre. Online, the best source of information is the **Friends of Algonquin Park** (www.algonquinpark.on.ca). **Ontario Parks** (www.ontarioparks.com) will give you an overview of the park facilities but doesn't provide as much detail.

Mobile phones do work in Algonquin Park, if you're within about three kilometers (1.9 miles) on either side of Highway 60. There are dead spots, though, and outside of this zone, don't count on picking up a phone signal.

Within the park, three stores sell camping supplies (including mosquito repellent, rain ponchos, and basic first aid) and a small selection of groceries. The **Portage Store** (KM 14.1) is on the west end of Highway 60 at Canoe Lake, the **Two Rivers Store** (KM 31.4) at the Lake of Two Rivers Campground is at roughly the midway point on Highway 60, and the **Opeongo Store** is to the east, a short drive north of KM 46.3.

GETTING THERE
By Car

Algonquin's West Gate is 45 kilometers (28 miles) east of Huntsville, via Highway 60. The

East Gate is five kilometers (three miles) west of the town of Whitney. From Toronto (270 kilometers, or 168 miles), the most direct, if most heavily trafficked, route is to take Highway 400 north to Highway 11 north, which will take you to Huntsville, where you can pick up Highway 60 to the West Gate.

An alternate route from Toronto takes you to the East Gate. Go east on Highway 401, then pick up Highway 115 into Peterborough; from there, take Highway 28 north to Bancroft, Highway 62 north to Maynooth, then Highway 127 north to Highway 60, which will bring you to the park's East Gate. While this route sounds more complicated, it's clearly marked; it's about 310 kilometers (193 miles) from the Toronto metropolitan area.

From Ottawa, pick up Highway 417/17 west to Highway 60, which will take you into the park. It's 240 kilometers (150 miles) from Ottawa to the East Gate.

You can buy gas at the Portage Store (KM 14.1, early May–mid-Oct.). Otherwise, the nearest gas stations are in Oxtongue Lake and Dwight west of the park and in Whitney to the east.

By Bus

Launched in 2010, the **Parkbus** (800/928-7101, www.parkbus.ca) provides direct bus service from Toronto to Algonquin. It's a nonprofit initiative designed to get people out of the city—and out of their cars. The bus runs on select weekends throughout the summer season. The bus departs from several points in Toronto, including 30 College St. (between Yonge and Church Streets, one block from the College subway station) and Dufferin Street, at Bloor Street West, which is at Dufferin station.

You can get off the bus at several points, including the Wolf Den Hostel near Oxtongue Lake, the West Gate, the Portage Store at Canoe Lake, Lake of Two Rivers Campground, Pog Lake, and the Algonquin Outfitters store

on Lake Opeongo. These locations either have accommodations (you can camp at Lake of Two Rivers or Pog Lake, or bunk at the Wolf Den), or they're departure points for outfitters who organize guided trips. The Parkbus works with several outfitters, so you can buy an all-inclusive trip, if you prefer.

If you're coming from Huntsville, there's another bus option that can take you to the park. **Hammond Transportation** (705/645-5431, www.hammondtransportation.com, one-way $36) runs a bus from Huntsville to Algonquin, on Mondays, Wednesdays, and Fridays from late June through August. The bus leaves the Huntsville depot at 1:15 P.M. and makes three stops: at Algonquin Outfitters on Oxtongue Lake (1:50 P.M.), at the Portage Store on Canoe Lake (2:00 P.M.), and at Lake of Two Rivers General Store, near the campground (2:15 P.M.). The return bus leaves Lake of Two Rivers at 2:30 P.M., the Portage Store at 2:45 P.M., and Algonquin Outfitters at 3 P.M., returning to Huntsville at 3:30 P.M. Since the bus operates only three times a week, you need to stay at least two days to catch the bus back to Huntsville. Still, it's a useful option if you're camping or going on a guided trip with one of these outfitters.

GETTING AROUND

There is no public transportation within Algonquin. If you arrive on the **Parkbus** (800/928-7101, www.parkbus.ca), you can camp at Lake of Two Rivers or Pog Lake, which are both centrally located and have hiking, cycling, and canoeing options nearby, so it's feasible to do without a car. You can also arrive by bus and do a canoeing or hiking trip that you've booked through an outfitter; the bus will drop you at one of several outfitters' locations.

Otherwise, unless you're comfortable bicycling or hiking long distances, you need a car to explore the park. The most convenient place to rent a car in the vicinity of the park is in Huntsville.

www.moon.com

DESTINATIONS | ACTIVITIES | BLOGS | MAPS | BOOKS

MOON.COM is ready to help plan your next trip! Filled with fresh trip ideas and strategies, author interviews, informative travel blogs, a detailed map library, and descriptions of all the Moon guidebooks, Moon.com is all you need to get out and explore the world—or even places in your own backyard. While at Moon.com, sign up for our monthly e-newsletter for updates on new releases, travel tips, and expert advice from our on-the-go Moon authors. As always, when you travel with Moon, expect an experience that is uncommon and truly unique.

KEEP UP WITH MOON ON FACEBOOK AND TWITTER
JOIN THE MOON PHOTO GROUP ON FLICKR

MAP SYMBOLS

▓▓▓ Expressway	◖ Highlight	✖ Airfield	♪ Golf Course
▒▒▒ Primary Road	○ City/Town	✈ Airport	▯ Parking Area
── Secondary Road	◉ State Capital	▲ Mountain	⬟ Archaeological Site
■ ■ ■ Unpaved Road	⊛ National Capital	✛ Unique Natural Feature	⬛ Church
- - - - - Trail	★ Point of Interest		⬛ Gas Station
·········· Ferry	● Accommodation	≋ Waterfall	Glacier
- - - - - Railroad	▼ Restaurant/Bar	⯅ Park	Mangrove
▓▓▓ Pedestrian Walkway	■ Other Location	▯ Trailhead	Reef
▭▭▭ Stairs	Λ Campground	⛷ Skiing Area	Swamp

CONVERSION TABLES

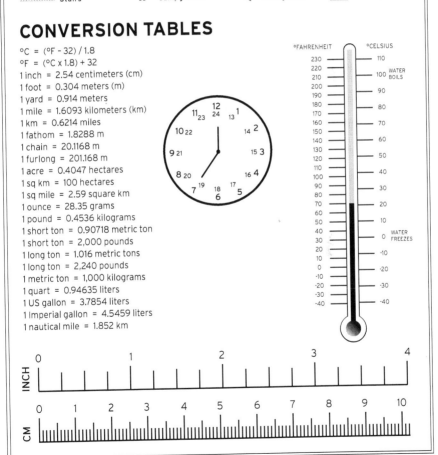

°C = (°F - 32) / 1.8
°F = (°C x 1.8) + 32
1 inch = 2.54 centimeters (cm)
1 foot = 0.304 meters (m)
1 yard = 0.914 meters
1 mile = 1.6093 kilometers (km)
1 km = 0.6214 miles
1 fathom = 1.8288 m
1 chain = 20.1168 m
1 furlong = 201.168 m
1 acre = 0.4047 hectares
1 sq km = 100 hectares
1 sq mile = 2.59 square km
1 ounce = 28.35 grams
1 pound = 0.4536 kilograms
1 short ton = 0.90718 metric ton
1 short ton = 2,000 pounds
1 long ton = 1.016 metric tons
1 long ton = 2,240 pounds
1 metric ton = 1,000 kilograms
1 quart = 0.94635 liters
1 US gallon = 3.7854 liters
1 Imperial gallon = 4.5459 liters
1 nautical mile = 1.852 km

MOON SPOTLIGHT GEORGIAN BAY
& COTTAGE COUNTRY
Avalon Travel
a member of the Perseus Books Group
1700 Fourth Street
Berkeley, CA 94710, USA
www.moon.com

Editor: Sabrina Young
Series Manager: Kathryn Ettinger
Copy Editor: Angela Buckley
Production and Graphics Coordinators: Tabitha Lahr,
    Kathryn Osgood
Cover Designer: Kathryn Osgood
Map Editor: Mike Morgenfeld
Cartographers: Chris Henrick, Kaitlin Jaffe, Andrea
    Butkovic

ISBN-13: 978-1-61238-557-0

Title page photo: touring Killarney Provincial Park by
canoe © Carolyn B. Heller

Printed in the United States.

KEEPING CURRENT

If you have a favorite gem you'd like to see included in the next edition, or see anything
that needs updating, clarification, or correction, please drop us a line. Send your com-
ments via email to feedback@moon.com, or use the address above.

ABOUT THE AUTHOR

Carolyn B. Heller

After moving to Canada in 2003, Carolyn B. Heller began exploring Ontario's outdoors, from the Bruce Peninsula's rocky shores to the pink cliffs of Killarney and the lakes and trails in Algonquin Provincial Park. A full-time travel, food, and feature writer, Carolyn has contributed to more than 50 travel and restaurant guides to destinations ranging from Canada to China. She's the author of the travel and relocation guide *Moon Living Abroad in Canada* and its companion website, www.livingabroadincanada.com. Her articles have appeared in publications including the *Los Angeles Times*, *Boston Globe*, *FamilyFun*, *Real Weddings*, and *Perceptive Travel*, as well as the book *Travelers' Tales Paris*.

Carolyn is an avid traveler and passionate food lover who has eaten on the streets, in fine restaurants, and everywhere in between in nearly 40 countries. A graduate of Brown University, she lives in Vancouver with her husband and twin daughters, where you can often find her trying out a new recipe, running on the beach, or struggling to learn Mandarin Chinese. Follow Carolyn's adventures at www.cbheller.com and on Twitter @CarolynBHeller.